TOURING ENGLAND
By Road and Byway

TOURING ENGLAND
BY ROAD AND BYWAY

By
SYDNEY R. JONES

Author and Artist of
"The Village Homes of England,"
"Old Houses in Holland," etc., etc.

This edition digitally re-mastered and
published by JM Classic Editions © 2007
Original text © Sydney R Jones 1927

ISBN 978-1-905217-61-8

All rights reserved. No part of this book subject
to copyright may be reproduced in any form or
by any means without prior permission in writing
from the publisher.

PREFACE

FOR a small island England contains much diversity of scenery and many distinctive and unrivalled features: green undulating landscapes, picturesque villages, old halls set in wide expanses of park, green lanes and footpaths, with many scenes rich in historical memories. But much of this is little known to English folk, and anything outside a few limited areas is rarely explored by visitors. It is the endeavour of this book by a series of specimen tours to act as a finger-post to some of these characteristics, and to provide directions by routes and maps, with illustrations from photographs and sketches. The tours given have been personally studied and recorded over a number of years of exploration by car or cycle, and on foot; it is hoped that they will be found helpful whatever means of progression is adopted. The method has been to avoid main roads and well-known routes, and some of the ways in hilly districts will be found arduous. The aim of this book being to aid in promoting the spirit of leisurely rambling, it is intended for the saunterer a-wheel or a-foot, rather than for the motorist who journeys between large centres at a maximum speed along main high-roads. Such tours may be multiplied almost endlessly, and one of the purposes is to provide a groundwork for further exploration by the tourist on his own account. There is no more profitable occupation than getting a grasp of the country-side by planning and working out with map and guide-book.

The limits set have involved the omission of many possible routes in pleasant districts, and the book must be considered as a miniature rather than a picture. As it is, much careful scheming has been necessary to get the information and the illustrations supplied within the limits of a handy volume for the pocket, and at a price that will appeal to all who care for touring. Inevitably many possible tours or centres have been omitted, as well as Scotland, Wales and Ireland; similarly the purpose of the book would be stultified and its price unduly enhanced if illustrations were made larger, and such features as a bibliography or historical notes included—these are outside its aim and method. If the volume proves helpful to the tourist there will be scope for further books of routes worked out with fuller description and illustration, and arranged under districts.

For Mr. Harry Batsford's suggestions, arising from an intimate acquaintance with England's country, to Mrs. Sydney Jones for carefully drawing all the maps, and to those who have gladly given corroborative evidence on roads, the author offers his grateful thanks. For additions to the author's set of photographs which, with the drawings, have been especially made for this book, acknowledgment is due to Messrs. J. Valentine & Sons: Plates II (No. 2); IV (No. 1), VII (No. 3), XIV, XXII (No. 2); Messrs. The Photochrom Co., Ltd.: Plates I (No. 1), IX (No. 2); Messrs. F. Frith & Co., Ltd.: Plates I (No. 2), VIII (No. 2), IX (No. 1), X (Nos. 1 & 3), XIII (No. 2), XX (No. 2), XXI (No. 1); Mr. J. H. Purcell: Plate XII (No. 1); Mr. G. Hepworth: Plate XIX (No. 3).

SYDNEY R. JONES.

May, 1927.

CONTENTS

	PAGE
PREFACE	v
INTRODUCTION	ix

DIVISION I—SOUTH-EASTERN :—
Introduction 1
Route 1. A Canterbury Pilgrimage . . 4
   ,,   2. Surrey Hills and the South Downs . 11
   ,,   3. Rural Essex and the Constable Country . 17
   ,,   4. By Thames and Chilterns into Hertfordshire 22

DIVISION II—SOUTH-WESTERN :—
Introduction 29
Route 5. Salisbury Plain and the New Forest . 33
   ,,   6. Somerset and Lyme Bay 38
   ,,   7. The Quantocks, Exmoor and Devon . . 42
   ,,   8. Cornwall 48

DIVISION III—THE MIDLANDS :—
Introduction 54
Route 9. The Washington Country and the Cotswolds 57
   ,, 10. From the Warwickshire Avon to the Wye . 63
   ,, 11. Across Mid England 68
   ,, 12. Cheshire, the Peak and the Dukeries . . 76

DIVISION IV—EASTERN :—
Introduction 82
Route 13. Old Suffolk Towns 85
   ,, 14. Norfolk and the Broads 89
   ,, 15. The Fen Country 95
   ,, 16. Lincolnshire Wolds and Lowlands . 100

DIVISION V—NORTHERN :—
Introduction 106
Route 17. Yorkshire Moors and Coast . . 108
   ,, 18. York to Lancaster 113
   ,, 19. Yorkshire Dales and the Lakes . . 118
   ,, 20. The Great Wall and the Border . . 122

INDEX TO TEXT AND ILLUSTRATIONS . . 129

INTRODUCTION

As a touring ground it is possible that England has not received the attention it deserves. Though its landscapes are soft and suave rather than grand, no country within comparatively small limits can offer more varied scenes of natural beauty, distinctive in character, and of their kind unsurpassed in Europe or the world over. Some parts of England are rugged and mountainous, others are quiet and almost tame, but this gentler type of scenery makes a deeper appeal to many. Nowhere does the scenery show more happily the effect of the continuous work of man, and nowhere does man's handiwork blend more pleasantly with the natural countryside. Both landscape and architecture express with trim hedges and well-set buildings that strong and widespread, yet never tyrannical, sense of order that is characteristic of the people. The villages, especially where unspoiled by modern methods, are extremely, indeed surprisingly, picturesque, and are thoroughly expressive of the local materials indigenous to each district. Foreign visitors who have penetrated into *real* England have always been struck by its ordered beauty, and its fresh greenery, which unlike that in southern and hotter lands persists from spring right through to the autumn fall of the leaf.

For more than a thousand years the beauty of England has been praised and recorded. Such early writers as Bede, Asser and William of Malmesbury, and discerning observers like Chaucer, Shakespeare and Milton, Evelyn, Goldsmith, Wordsworth, Hazlitt, Washington Irving, Borrow, Emerson, Ruskin, Richard Jefferies, and Henry James, have furnished a continuous theme of praise and admiration

INTRODUCTION

down the centuries, and this has been continued into our own day by such enthusiasts as Thomas Hardy and Rudyard Kipling, to be carried forward quite lately by John Drinkwater, Karel Capek and the Rt. Hon. Stanley Baldwin. Although a surfeit of applause is not always a true indication of excellence, this subject of so much praise is no less beautiful than it has been represented.

This volume is intended to indicate where some of England's attractions lie, and how they may be reached. The tours are schemed to cover the country in the following manner. The map of England is split into five divisions, viz., South-eastern, South-western, Midland, Eastern, and Northern. Within each division four routes are arranged, varying in length from 120 to something over 200 miles; devised to connect one with another, they suggest tours of greater distances, and circuits through some of the most picturesque districts of England. Divisions and routes are given on the diagram on page viii, and they are described in detail under their separate headings. Each of these five district divisions has a brief introduction on characteristics and chief features, with a glance at the part it has played in English history. The four routes that follow are each provided with a map of the tour and illustrations of typical scenes and villages from photographs and the author's sketches. Though the description of every route is necessarily short, an endeavour has been made to touch briefly on its scenery and features of interest in country, hamlet and town. Main routes have been consistently and it is hoped beneficially avoided. Inasmuch as very many charming ways are available these routes must be regarded as sample ones only, capable of being developed or multiplied tenfold. Sometimes keeping to highways, and often turning along minor roads and winding lanes, they are all suitable for motorists who, wishing to forsake well-known beaten tracks, are prepared to follow their maps into less frequented parts. Cyclists will improve on the routes by using more lanes, and for

INTRODUCTION　　　　　　　　　　　　　　xi

walkers there are always field paths and green tracks. All who travel on wheels also have endless opportunities for making pedestian detours, and some of the points where such may be taken advantageously are indicated in the text.

Covering but a small area, the face of the country is remarkably diversified with its gardens, hedgerows, green pastures, orchards, brooks, woods, and countless valleys watered by rivers. Smooth rounded downs and shady combes of the south and the west contrast with eastern flat

LEWES AND THE SOUTH DOWNS.

lands divided by dykes. Midland wolds and low hills lead up to the heathery moors of the north, and highest of all, framing lakes and waterfalls, rise the northern mountains, down whose steep slopes rapid streams leap from rock to rock. The sea encloses all, ebbing and flowing over stretches of sand, or breaking at the foot of white chalk cliffs and rugged headlands.

Richly endowed by nature, it should be realised that the general scene has been determined in part by human influences. Systems of ownership and occupation of land, long-established practices in husbandry, the customs and usages of country life, and a constant need of communication from place to place, have moulded the landscape into its present form. Immemorial oak trees mark the demesne of a feudal baron. Commons, traces of open fields, or perhaps an old mill-race, survive as bequests of a manorial system. Sometimes our imagination is touched by the sight of still water which proves to be a moat. Then we may light upon a causeway made by the monks, a riverside bed of withies telling of rural industry, a long avenue of beeches leading to the pedimented front of a mansion. Here is a spot where wheat has been grown for generations; the sheep-walks on those downs are older than one can tell; that patchwork of hedges and green has long been known as fine grazing land. Maybe the straight road we are travelling on was first planned by Julius Agricola, and near to the cross-roads, where coaches used to change horses, a yet older way goes over a chalk hill in the form of a green and white track.

Countless generations of men have added other features to the countryside which, in their many forms, reveal the nation's past. Stones and earthworks recall times before history was recorded, and Britons, Romans, Saxons, Danes and Normans have all left visible marks. The course of political, military, and ecclesiastical events over a very long period, as well as the everyday life of the people, is recalled by many buildings, by castles, cathedrals and churches, homes of great families and squires, guildhalls, markets, houses in country towns, farms and cottages. So beautiful are many of these works, and so well do they harmonise with the natural settings in which they stand, that they constitute one of the greatest charms of the English scene. Hardly less pleasant are the various kinds of communicating ways that have been gradually developed, joining village to village, town to town, or giving through routes to distant parts. Each type has its peculiar attractions. We admire the generous width of the old highways at, say, Henley-in-Arden and Marlborough, and applaud the direct purpose of a road like Ermine Street from Lincoln, or Wat-

INTRODUCTION

ling Street in Staffordshire, running straight as an arrow to its goal. Such towns as Coventry, Shrewsbury, and York still preserve the lines of their mediæval streets. Byways and lanes show the varied loveliness of hedgerow, wood, and distance. Footpaths hold some of the greatest delights, and those trackways that were formed when men first set out to discover England are good to traverse and full of human meaning. Wherever the tourist looks—in the

HORNING, NORFOLK.

Clun Valley road, the upper reaches of the Wharfe, the tracks on the Downs and the Quantocks, in fields above Haddon and Montacute, beside Hickling Broad, and in a thousand other directions—he will find his own favoured retreats.

A splendid system of highways, one of the best in the world, makes the discovery of England a much simpler matter than it was formerly. Fine roads, well adapted for all kinds of wheeled traffic, lead everywhere. The surface of by-roads and lanes nowadays is generally remarkably good, and many of the narrow ways that often look unpromising on the map give far better going than they promise. Signposts are numerous. Policemen on point duty and A.A. scouts willingly render help in finding the way.

Intimately connected with the roads is the question of accommodation for meals and sleeping. This is a subject on which experienced travellers advise only with diffidence, for round English inns criticism has raged for centuries. On them have been delightful eulogies by Shenstone and Washington Irving, praise and complaints from Doctor Johnson, Hazlitt's thoughts on enviable hours spent " over a bottle of sherry and a cold chicken," Lamb's whimsical story of the Quakers' unpaid reckoning at Andover, and the eighteenth-century quip from Newbury :—

> " The famous inn at Speenhamland
> That stands below the hill,
> May well be called the Pelican
> From its enormous bill."

After a long period of eclipse due to the introduction of railways country hotels once more have vast opportunities waiting at their doors, for users of the road are now more numerous than in the palmiest days of the coaching era. The demand created by increased road travel has improved supply, and a number of excellent hostelries are to be found in various parts of England. Lists of hotels throughout the country are issued by the Royal Automobile Club, the Automobile Association, the Cyclists' Touring Club and kindred organisations, the People's Refreshment House Association, and Public House Trusts in sundry counties. Then there are village inns, unknown to fame and not ordinarily catering for tourists, within whose hospitable parlours some of the best experiences are sometimes gained. In the supply of meals hotel-keepers generally have certainly not kept abreast of the times by offering the extravagant and often unwanted table d'hote, or the inevitable cold meat and pickles, at high prices. There is a real need for a group

INTRODUCTION

of houses that will cater for people of moderate means, giving simple and good accommodation at reasonable cost. For their own edification and profit landlords might well study the excellent services their Continental neighbours render to tourists. Meals taken in the open can be delightful whenever the weather is fine and sunny. It is a capital idea when travelling from place to place to carry a thermos flask, purchase locally sufficient provisions for the day, and picnic just where fancy dictates. For hardy souls who appreciate the glories of early morning, rare sights of wild life, and fine runs on deserted roads, an occasional night spent in a closed car or portable tent is not to be despised.

The possibilities and charm of private lodgings ought to be better known. Although not invariably good, such quarters often surprise by their excellence. While few villages in England do not offer house and cottage accommodation, there is difficulty in locating it; information can usually be obtained on enquiry at post offices, police and railway stations, and on occasions, through letters to clergymen. The railway companies also publish detailed lists of apartments and farm-house rooms.

With signposts and maps tourists will find the remotest places. Everyone should cultivate the ability to read maps intelligently, for these printed documents, suggesting and meaning so much, add to pleasure on the way. By contours and spot-heights we know that here is a hill, there a valley; curves of blue or black really mean gleaming waters; radiating parallel lines, now straight, now winding, indicate the history of roads; and there is a wealth of suggestion in place-names. Maps published by the Ordnance Survey or John Bartholomew are the best to use. Those to the scale of four miles to an inch are good for the main basis of touring, as each sheet covers an area sufficiently large to enable one to visualise wide stretches of country. More detailed information is provided by the two miles to an inch maps, which give an ideal scale for ordinary purposes. To find the way through unknown country without touching highways, and for really careful exploration, nothing is better than the Ordnance maps to the scale of one mile to the inch. Contour books giving the gradients of roads also have their uses, and they are published to embrace England by sections. When travelling away from the north point, that is, from north to south, practice brings the knack of reading a map in reverse, or more helpfully, upside-down. When a halt is made, objects of interest in all directions will be revealed with the aid of the map: after it has been placed in correct relation to the points of the compass, imaginary sight lines from the position of observation will enable every distant feature to be identified. In this connection a pocket compass is a desirable possession; there is also the rough and ready method of finding a bearing by pointing the hour-hand of a watch to the sun, the south being midway between it and the figure of twelve o'clock.

To mark maps is to give them a personal value, at the same time adding to them intimate information such as no guide books will give. Wherever the traveller's interest or curiosity has been aroused, the place can be recorded by a sign on the map. Thus, the location of a manor-house can be shown by an M, a church by a C, supplemented by a figure (such as 14) denoting the century to which it mainly belongs; a remarkable castle, stretch of road, park or hill, is underlined, and a notable village bears a X. To do this means little trouble at the end of a tour, and dark blue ink shews best. The signs, which can be extended indefinitely, transform maps into really valuable documents, and they ensure the remembrance of things that otherwise might be forgotten and never again visited.

The usefulness of maps is further increased if the main geological divisions of the country are marked on them in red or blue pencil. Geology means more to the tourist than is commonly recognised. The structure of the earth has partly determined the quality of roads and landscape;

INTRODUCTION

it has affected the course of history, and has been an influence in developing human character. It was the chalky nature of the hills that fixed the routes of the earliest trackways, bold eminences gave sites for camps and castles, and natural features have always reacted on the temperament of the people. As the tourist comes down from the Pennines in Derbyshire, crosses the Midland Plain, mounts the

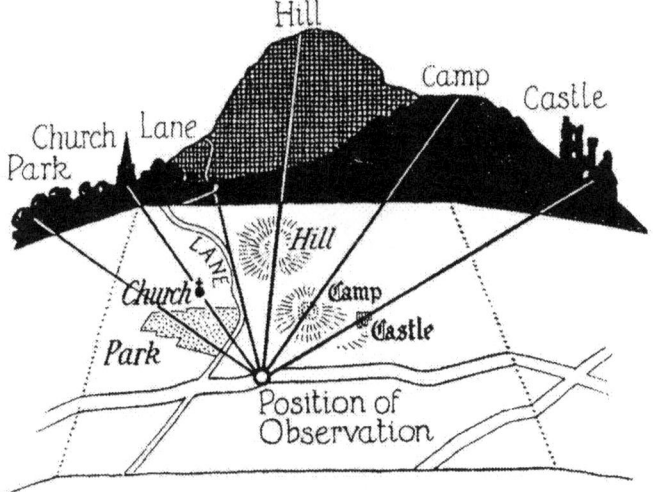

Cotswolds at Broadway, descends from Burford into the Vale of the White Horse, and makes his way over the Berkshire Downs and the Chilterns into the Weald of Kent, or bears west to Dorset and Devon, he is conscious of many changes in scene and architecture. Rugged mountains of limestone, level plains of sandstone, oolitic heights, and rounded downs and hills of chalk are reached and passed in turn. The type of architecture constantly differs as each geological formation is gained. Massive stone buildings give place to those of timber, erected from the oak trees that grew on the sandstone. Villages

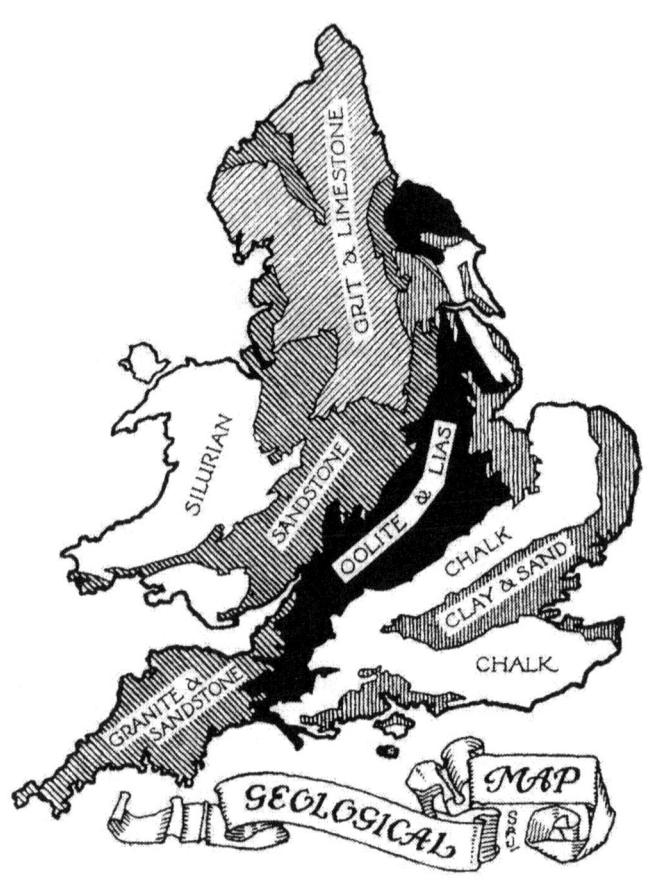

INTRODUCTION

built of local oolite are succeeded by white plaster cottages. In other places are magnificent abbeys and churches developed from freestone or flint. Old gables and twisted chimneys are traceable to beds of clay that gave material for brickmaking, and where granite abounds the architecture betrays the influence of geological conditions. With maps marked to indicate geology, features such as these will be quickly recognised by the tourist as he travels from formation to formation, through the valleys and over the hillsides of England.

Planned to include characteristic scenery, these tours also reveal points suggestive of the story and meaning of the country, touching now and again places and things that probably will not remain for future generations to see. These last words refer to new conditions, the product of quite recent years. The present century has witnessed events of far-reaching consequence which have affected social and economic life, brought changes to the mental outlook of the people, and in some measure altered the aspect of the countryside. The old type of villager has become almost extinct; the division of large estates has meant a revolution in the ownership of land. The nineteenth century added a vast quantity of ugly and unpleasant building, and the changes of the present day are even more radical. Old cottages give place to housing schemes, villas and bungalows, and roadside advertisements, petrol pumps and similar disfigurements are becoming common. Inevitable road improvements often involve cutting away pleasant hedges and groups of old trees, and the great arterial roads, often cutting through virgin soil, have a hard efficiency entirely different from the picturesque and intimate winding ways of earlier times. Some may deplore these changes, others may welcome them as signs of progress; all will rejoice in attempts to brighten village life and the improved communications brought about by the spread of motor traffic in the country. But the

English country of the future will doubtless be different from that of the past. With so much still remaining that is unique in its beauty, the operations of The National Trust, and the newly-formed Council for the Preservation of Rural England, are particularly opportune, while the movements which has for their aims "See England" and "Come to Britain" are especially full of meaning at the present time.

> "Strait mine eye hath caught new pleasures
> Whilst the landskip round it measures;
> Russet lawns, and fallows gray,
> Where the nibbling flocks do stray;
> Mountains on whose barren breast
> The labouring clouds do often rest;
> Meadows trim with daisies pied
> Shallow brooks, and rivers wide;
> Towers and battlements it sees
> Bosomed high in tufted trees."
>
> *L'Allegro.*

THE OUSE AT HOLYWELL.

PLATE I.

Dunster and the Bristol Channel

Pitch Hill, View from Holmbury Hill.

DIVISION I
SOUTH-EASTERN ENGLAND

(Shewn on Map, facing Introduction, p. viii).

THIS part of England, especially interesting to those who sojourn or make their homes in the neighbourhood of London, is bounded by the coastline from Ipswich to Southampton; by roads connecting Southampton, Andover and Newbury; and by a line passing from Newbury, through Watlington, Aylesbury, Bedford and Cambridge, to Ipswich. With London as its centre, this area includes the earlier stages of many of the great roads of history, which radiate from the metropolis to the north, south, east and west—to Dover, Brighton and Portsmouth, to Exeter and Bath, to Holyhead, York, Norwich, and elsewhere. In between the great roads are important direct and cross routes, linked up by innumerable byways. Petrol and other vehicles make road traffic heavy over a very wide district bordering the capital city, but it is surprising how many quiet rural ways can be found by all who will take the trouble to read their maps intelligently. Hilly roads abound in the country of the Chilterns, those of the Weald and the heights of Sussex and Kent are by no means flat, and the ground surfaces of Hertfordshire and north Essex are undulating. Towards the eastern coastline, and round the mouth of the Thames, a percentage of the highways and lanes are perfectly level. Loose flints in the chalk districts, and greasy surfaces in wet weather where clay is prevalent, are the main difficulties of travel on the byroads. The Downs and the Chiltern Hills provide many delightful tracks, and the field paths throughout Kent, Sussex, Buckinghamshire and Hertfordshire are particularly beautiful.

The main geological systems of the district are simple. Chalk, Greensand, and Wealden formations extend continuously from the Straits of Dover towards Hampshire, there is chalk in the Chilterns, Hertfordshire, and north Essex, while the clays and sands of the Thames Valley and Essex intervene. These systems are diversified in places by local subdivisions. The scenery in south-eastern England combines variety with richness. The beauties of the Weald, that justly deserves its appellation " the garden of England," vie with the leafiness of homely Hertfordshire. Relics of great woodlands, which are many, are to be seen particularly well in St. Leonard's and Ashdown Forests, round Haslemere, in the neighbourhood of Windsor Great Park, at Woolmer and Bere in Hampshire, and in Epping Forest and western Essex. The hills of the Chilterns, and the North and South Downs, with their arrays of beech and pine, present scenes of enduring charm at all seasons of the year. There is peculiar attraction in Romney Marsh, Thanet, and the low-lying Essex coast; noble cliffs rise where the Downs meet the Kent and Sussex sea; river valleys, like those of the Stour, the upper Medway, the Rother, and the Arun, give real English landscapes; while the Thames, winding between open pastures and banks of deep wood, and flowing past old-world towns, villages, and quiet backwaters, brings to this south-eastern district some of its most precious jewels.

Memories of people and events crowd the roads and byways of this corner of England. Reminders of times past recall almost every stage of the country's history from the earliest to most recent times. The chalk hills of the Downs and the Chilterns, capable of providing reasonably hard and dry going not impeded by insurmountable natural obstacles of wood and water, gave lines of communication to British tribes, whose trackways may yet be traced on the Sussex Downs, along the Pilgrim's Way, and under the Buckingham and Bedfordshire hills. The walls of Chichester, St. Albans, and the first Roman colony of Colchester, the remains at Richborough in Kent, at Silchester near Reading, and at Bignor in Sussex, together with other evidences in many places, bring to mind the period of the Roman occupation, that was first foreshadowed by the landing of Julius Cæsar at

INTRODUCTION 3

Walmer in Kent. Travellers of to-day, as they go from Brentford to Colchester, through Staines, by Canterbury and Rochester, or follow the approximate lines of Ermine Street through Ware and Royston, Watling Street by Edgware and Dunstable, and Stane Street from Dorking to Chichester, may gratefully remember those Roman engineers who first developed England's great road system. A multitude of subsequent events are associated with names on the map—Saxon kings reigning at Winchester; William the Conqueror landing at Pevensey; pilgrims making pleasant summer journeys to Canterbury's shrine; battles at Lewes and Barnet; Henry V leaving the gates of Southampton for Agincourt; royal huntings in the forests; Wat Tylers' rebels surging through Kent to Blackheath; Jack Cade's end at Cade Street, near Heathfield in Sussex; admirals embarking at Portsmouth and the Cinque Ports; Gunpowder Plotters fleeing through St. Albans and Dunstable; Cromwell battering Basing House; Charles II's escape over the Hampshire and Sussex Downs to Brighton and the sea; and seventeenth, eighteenth, and early nineteenth century society going by road to Tunbridge Wells, Brighton, and Bath. Further place-names are connected with progresses innumerable made by conspicuous and insignificant people, by kings and queens, prelates and statesmen, Sussex iron-masters and martyrs, coachmen, Regency bucks, highwaymen and smugglers. Other souls, too, especially belong to this district of England so rich in associations. Shades of Chaucer, Marlowe, Shakespeare, Scott and Dickens rub shoulders on the Dover Road. Thackeray is of the Brighton Road. Pepys paid his reckonings on his way to Portsmouth, Reading and Cambridge. Gilbert White patiently watched in the Hampshire village of Selborne, Isaac Walton caught fish in the Lea under Amwell Hill, Charles Lamb loved his Widford and Wheathampstead country, Constable revealed the beauty of the Stour valley, and Turner painted at Petworth.

The natural scene of hill, and dale, and pastoral landscape, is studded with pretty villages and country towns which yet remain unspoiled. Such villages are too numerous to mention. The list of small towns includes Sandwich, Rye, Cranbrook, Lewes, Steyning, Arundel, Petworth, Midhurst,

Farnham, Odiham, Alton, Bishops Waltham, and Titchfield, to the south of the Thames, while north of the river are Watlington, Chesham, Wheathampstead, Ware, Thaxted, Clare, Nayland, and Maldon. Throughout the Weald, and on the undulating lands of Kent, Surrey, Sussex, and the Hampshire border, the groups of rural buildings shew harmonious combinations of timbering, hanging tiles, weatherboarding and plaster. Over them rise the picturesque oast-houses and occasional windmills. There is good work in brick and flint between Reading, High Wycombe, and Chesham, as well as in eastern Kent. Hertfordshire and north Essex are notable for their plasterwork, and eastern Essex is full of timber-framed houses and old brickwork. Within the area stand the famous cathedrals of Canterbury, Chichester, Winchester, and St. Albans, castles and houses such as Penshurst, Leeds, and Ightham Mote in Kent, Hurstmonceux and Bodiam in Sussex, Crowhurst Place in Surrey, Ockwells in Berkshire, Audley End and Layer Marney in Essex, and a wealth of smaller buildings displaying fine architecture.

ROUTE 1

ALTHOUGH Canterbury is the midway goal of this journey, it will be reached by a much more circuitous way than that followed by Chaucer's famous company. But the roads trodden by the pilgrims of bygone days will be encountered now and again. To accord with immemorial tradition, the start should be made from a " gentil hostelrye " on that very ancient highway out of London to south-east England, the Borough High Street. This pilgrimage, however, commences from Edenbridge, which may be approached from London by Westerham.

On the far side of the bridge, in Edenbridge, a left turning goes by Hever church and castle gateway, through Bow Beach, Chiddingstone village and, past the signposts, to Penshurst Park. This way at once dips into a homely and intimate stretch of Kent, sheltered from the north by a fine line of Downs. It is intersected by winding lanes and little

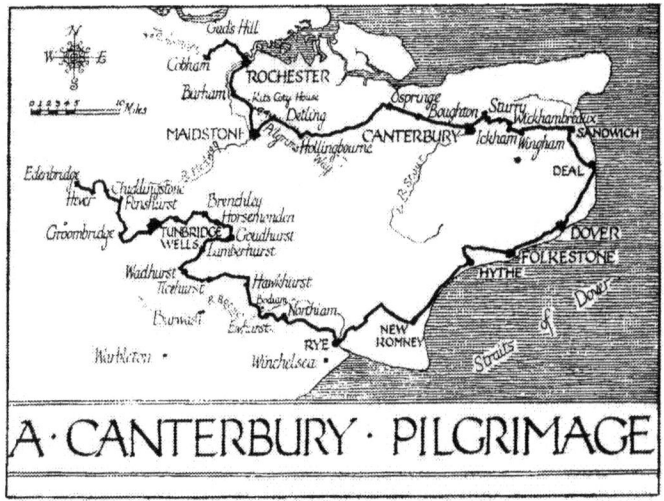

A·CANTERBURY · PILGRIMAGE

valleys full of fruit trees; from the higher ground is constantly seen a wide expanse of fertile vale bounded by distant wooded hills. There are villages partly hidden by trees, oast-houses, and the narrow green aisles of the hop gardens that are enlivened, in August and September, by groups of hop-pickers, who live and camp around in gipsy fashion. The timbered and tile-hung rural buildings, surrounded by flowers, give an added richness to the scene. Chiddingstone shews a particularly beautiful group, and after passing along the hillside road, lined with bracken, and descending into Penshurst, much will be found to please the eye. For Penshurst is delightful in itself—splendid, too, in its memories of Queen Elizabeth, the Earl of Leicester, and Sir Philip Sidney. By the old cottages, and under the churchyard arch, leads to the green levels of the park and the massive crenellated walls and towers of Penshurst Place.

Leaving Penshurst by the road of entry, the route is continued straight on, up the luxuriant Medway valley. Half-a-mile short of Langton a turning leads steeply down to Groombridge, where cottages and church are ranged round a sloping green. Behind the church, and approached by a footpath, is Groombridge Place, an outstanding example of the dignified architecture of Wren's time. From the foot of the village by the Eridge road, and bearing left past the railway bridge, is the prettiest way imaginable to Tunbridge Wells, past pines and bracken and heather, and under the High Rocks. The fashionable and royal days of Tunbridge Wells are no more, but the greenery and arcades of the Pantiles remain.

A fine stretch of the Hastings highway leaves Tunbridge Wells at the crest of the hill past the Central Station. Beyond Pembury, where the distances appear away to the north and south, a signpost directs to Brenchley. Further on is Horsmonden, then Goudhurst, perched high on a green slope. This borderland of Kent and Sussex is the country of the "hursts," marked some way on by Lamberhurst, Wadhurst, Ticehurst, and Hawkhurst. It abounds in little hills, and there are many trees, remnants of the forests that provided fuel for the Wealden iron industry when Sussex was England's "Black Country." Then the county supplied Edward II with horseshoes, and Queen Elizabeth with cannons. Inside many of the village dwellings are yet to be seen iron firebacks, dogs, and hearth and domestic implements. Iron grave-slabs can be found in the churchyards—there is a remarkable collection of them at Wadhurst—and placenames, such as Ashburnham Furnace, recall the vanished industry. Particularly good and abundant are the old houses and cottages fashioned in oak, plaster, tile-hanging and weather-boarding. Several of them are notable—Church House and Pattenden at Goudhurst, Shoyswell near Ticehurst, Hawkhurst Place, and to the south, the houses of Burwash and the rare Warbleton Priory.

Bodiam Castle, moated and ruined, is approached by a left turning from the main road, two miles past Hawkhurst. Winding lanes lead over the River Rother, through Ewhurst, to Northiam, a delectable spot possessing the old mansion of Brickwall, Great Dixter, Strawberry Hole, and Queen Elizabeth's Oak, under which her Majesty rested and feasted, and changed her shoes in 1573. It is but a few miles to Rye. This little town is a place apart. Obviously it has

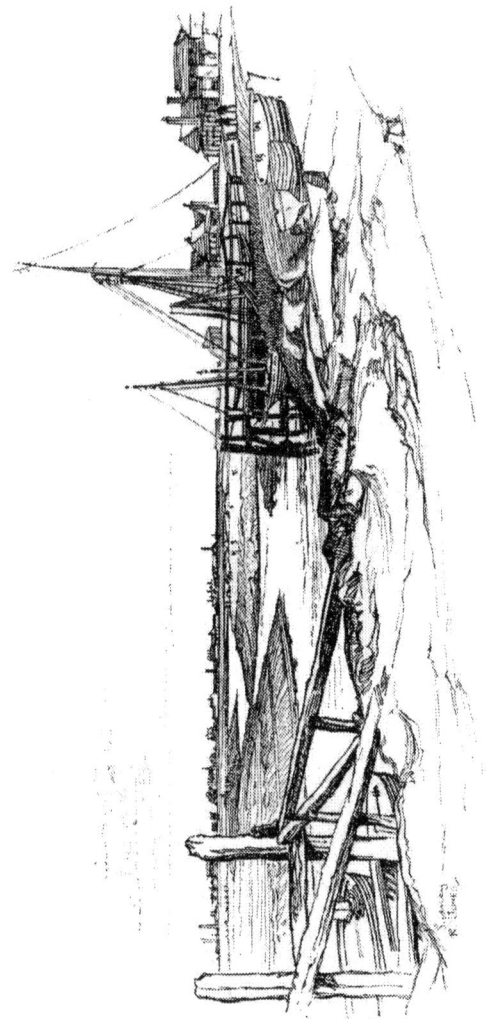

RYE HARBOUR.

been "found"—everything is so well done, and art blossoms strongly on casement curtains—but even so, it has not been spoiled. Not elsewhere in England is there to be seen anything better than Rye's cobbled streets and byways, or its assemblage of old walls and bright roofs, throned on a sandstone bluff rising abruptly from a level plain. They tell of the port's historic days, when its shipping, and smugglers too, were known far and wide. Then catastrophe came; the sea retired; the port was no more. Now only a stretch of sea is visible from the view-points between the Land Gate, the Ypres Tower, and Watchbell Street, and it breaks on the golden sands beyond Rye Harbour. Winchelsea, a little more than two miles distant, is both like and unlike Rye. It is high on a rock, is entirely of the past, and the sea no longer washes its eastern cliff. But it is greener, more sylvan, than its sister town. The spirit of the Middle Ages seems to have triumphed over the forces of decay, abiding still where stones have fallen. Guarded by mediæval gateways, and partly encircled by ruined town walls, this phantom of a great past peacefully continues, beautiful in its aloofness, a place of lovely buildings set among flowers and trees.

On leaving Rye for New Romney, the marsh road leads to the seaside route for Hythe, where a left turning follows the cliffs to Folkestone, Dover, and up the hill past the castle to the old ports of Deal and Sandwich, both picturesque aggregations of weathered brickwork, shewing gables and other features attributable to the influence of the Dutchmen and Flemings who, long ago, settled in this breezy, open country of Kent. Near the colourful gatehouse of Sandwich the Canterbury road turns inland. At the village of Wingham, lanes deviate to the right through a chain of little country places, all worth seeing—Ickham, Wickhambreaux, Fordwich, and Sturry. From the last-named village the city of the shrine of Thomas à Becket is quickly gained.

In Canterbury High Street, and to the right and left of it, the modern sojourner will find many things that earlier pilgrims saw—something of mediævalism, evidences of romance and history, bright colour, and if the day be calm and sunny, clear reflections in the little river Stour. Outside the great West Gate the road keeps to the line that has been

THE PILGRIM'S WAY NEAR KIT'S COTY HOUSE.

taken, at one time or another, by an endless throng of historical figures; crowded with the memories of personages and events of all ages, this Dover Road is rich above all others in associations. After Harbledown, "under the blee in Canterbury way," and past Boughton Hill, a turning on the left, at Ospringe, leads through the gardens of Kent until it drops down a steep hill into the old, old village street of Hollingbourne. Opposite the King's Head inn a signpost directs to Thurnham—and adventure. Here to the northwest and south-east runs that earliest of trackways, the Pilgrim's Way, devised by men who lived before the days of recorded time to connect the Channel coast with that first centre of communications, Salisbury Plain. Of all material things made by mankind, roads are the most permanent, and from Hollingbourne may be traced for miles a chalk track whose origin was already lost in the mists of antiquity when the first pilgrims to Canterbury used it. This, too, is a most beautiful Way. Sometimes it winds as a mere green and white track, sunken and enclosed, and almost screened from the sky by bushes; in places it follows the curves of open slopes; and now and again it appears as a modernised road. Above the Way there are always hills capped with woods, and old thorns, and bright patches of exposed chalk; below, red roofs and tapering oast-houses are partially hidden by orchards and high trees.

The Pilgrim's Way can be followed by a fairly good road to Detling. Between that point and the Maidstone-Chatham highway—a most romantic section—the track can be recommended only to the most efficient of motorists, though it is ideal for walking, and possible for cycling. An alternative route, however, goes to the left at Detling for Maidstone. Thence, by the Chatham road and three miles out, the Pilgrim's Way can be seen to the right and left, near to a tarred cottage and a large garage sign. Shortly ahead, down a left turning and opposite the Rochester signpost, is the stile and footpath leading to the prehistoric stones of Kit's Coty House. Here the Pilgrim's Way becomes the road to Burham, before it finally turns westwards for Winchester.

Rochester, above all things the city of Charles Dickens, is

PLATE III.

FORDWICH AND THE STOUR.

THE WAY TO THE FERRY, BURHAM.

PLATE IV.

COLDHARBOUR, LEITH HILL.

HARTFIELD, ASHDOWN FOREST

reached by the wide vale of the Medway. Quaint nooks and corners, and seared brick houses, combined in picturesque array round the cathedral and castle, are haunted by memories of the novelist. The river crossing also, and the ascent up to Gad's Hill beyond, are pre-eminently Dickensian stretches of road. The Falstaff Inn at the top of the hill recalls a Shakespearean scene. Opposite to it, an undulating lane leads the traveller to the woods of Cobham Park, a distant view of the Elizabethan hall, and Cobham village, well worth seeing for its church, college almshouses, and famous Leather Bottle inn, before rejoining the London highway.

ROUTE 2

DORKING, originally a Roman Camp on Stane Street which came up from Chichester and Pulborough by way of Leith Hill, is a pleasant little town in the heart of the Surrey hills. At the end of the main street the Horsham road, running south, quickly gives a branch way to Coldharbour and Leith Hill, two high points that may be reached only by a long upward climb. As the ascent is made, one obtains an excellent introduction to some of the best scenery Surrey can offer. The road banks are full of mosses and are overhung by trees; coppices and bracken cover the near slopes, pines and firs bring shapely silhouettes to the eminences, and away to the west hills succeed one another until they are lost in purple distances. Coldharbour reached, an enormous panorama over the Weald comes into view, to be seen even more advantageously from the adjacent summit of Leith Hill. Straight on, the hard road continues by a wonderful hillside way, closed in on either side by fine specimens of beech, pine, holly, and birch, rising from bracken undergrowth. Right down into Abinger this character of scene is maintained.

Just before Abinger church a pretty sunken lane leads down, leftwards, to the watered hollow of Sutton, situated below the spurs of Holmbury Hill. Twisting left, and between timbered cottages, a lovely valley road, first skirting

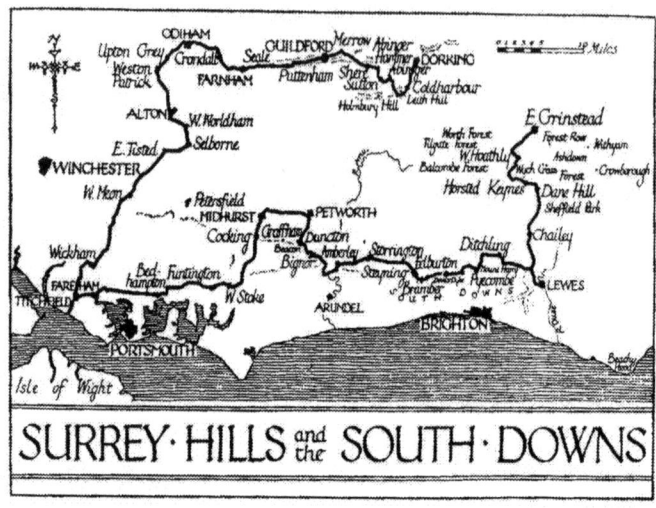

SURREY·HILLS and the SOUTH·DOWNS

Crossways, one of Surrey's finest groups of mellow brickwork and weather-boarding, eventually reaches the open greens and rippling waters of Abinger Hammer. Shere, one of the many "prettiest villages in England," is not far beyond. Short of Albury, a steep rise to the right crosses the hills and the Pilgrim's Way for Merrow and Guildford. Although new buildings and motors have come since Cobbett saw Guildford, his description of the town and environs, "the most agreeable and most happy-looking that I ever saw in my life," is still very near the truth. It is a bright, cheerful place when the sun shines on the castle ruins and Archbishop Abbot's Hospital, and over neighbouring meadows and downs. High Street, with its clock projecting from a seventeenth-century Town Hall, and also full of good things reminiscent of days when notable travellers and Portsmouth coaches came this way, is picturesque indeed.

After a climb of two miles from the bottom of Guildford High Street, superb views from the Hog's Back are obtained. Midway along the ridge a left-hand turning, for Puttenham, reaches the valley road that goes, as pilgrims went, by Seale to Farnham. This town, like several others hereabout, has preserved something of its old-time dignity. Quiet streets of solid brick houses, with eaves projecting above pilasters, doorway pediments, flights of steps, and delicate wrought ironwork, recall those earlier occupants who wore brocaded satins, knee breeches, and powdered wigs, took snuff, and read *Clarissa*. Castle Street and West Street wear just this

SELBORNE FROM THE ZIGZAG.

air, and further on, in the streets of Odiham and Alton, similar suggestions of centuries past jog the memory. In between these towns, after the ascent towards Crondall has been made, there are smooth undulations and patches of wood encircling villages like those of Upton Grey and Weston Patrick. Within reach of such peaceful places, and amidst tranquil Hampshire scenes, it is fitting that Gilbert White should have made his home, patiently to pursue those observations that are enshrined for all time in *The Natural History of Selborne*. His village, approached from Alton by way of West Worldham, "consists of one single straggling street, in a sheltered vale, and running parallel to the Hanger." All lovers of White's charming letters may still climb to the beeches of the "long hanging wood" and see the cottages and houses spread out below, may view "The Wakes," "The Plestor," and the ancient yew in the churchyard, and penetrate into rocky hollow lanes, "that delight the naturalist with their various botany."

Lanes connect Selborne with the Fareham road, which is undulating from East Tisted until it drops down to West Meon and the Meon valley. This valley way, and the districts to the east and the west of it from Petersfield to Winchester, are good exploring country on account of the quality of the villages, the ever-present feeling of remoteness from modernism, and the villagers themselves, who have developed from a Saxon ancestry. At Wickham, the right-hand turning for Bishops Waltham gives a branch to the left for sleepy old Titchfield, whose ancient greatness is now recalled only by the splendid ruins of Place House, and by the tombs in the church. Fareham, to the east, is a typical and bright small Hampshire town; after a sharp left turn for the church, the first turning on the right gives lovely views from the top of Portsdown. To the left of the level crossing, past Bedhampton and just short of Havant, lanes south of Rowlands Castle lead through Funtington and West Stoke to the Midhurst route that rises up the Downs. Over Cocking, wonderful scenery abounds among the hill slopes, and in the woodlands of East Dean and West Dean. Extending to the right and left are broad downs, regular hollows, and the shapely chalk ridges along which Charles II came in his flight from Worcester field. Here, from the summits of smooth hills, are to be seen those delicate combinations of vista, and distance, and joyous landscape, that bring to the Down country its abiding charm.

Midhurst, comparatively lowly placed, is a venerable town of much attraction, as all will find who linger in its gabled streets, or watch the lessening evening light enshroud in mystery the Tudor ruins of Cowdray. The forward direction from Midhurst is so full of beauty and interest, halts innumerable can be made—in the shady glades of Cowdray deer park, among Petworth's old-fashioned houses, and at

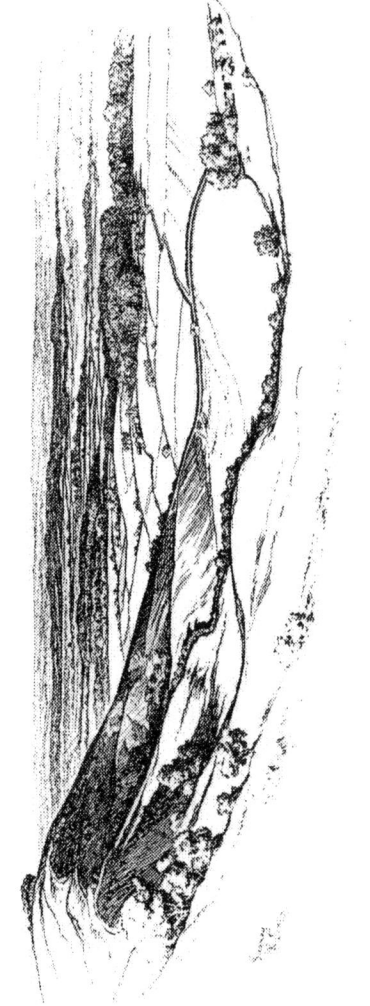

THE DOWNS AND THE WEALD, MOUNT HARRY.

Duncton, for the ascent to the green track on the hills above Wool Lavington and Graffham. On winding leftwards round Duncton Beacon there are reached, in turn, the relics of the Roman villa at Bignor, lying just where Stane Street sweeps down from Bignor Hill, the Arundel road (leading to the wonderful park of Arundel Castle), and an easterly route, over old Houghton bridge and by Amberley Castle, to Storrington, Steyning, Bramber, Beeding, Edburton, Poynings, Pyecombe, Ditchling, and Lewes. This route shews Sussex at its best. The gracious lines of the Downs, rising high at such points as Chanctonbury Ring, Devil's Dyke, and Ditchling Beacon, are never absent. Sheep feeding, fine horses and huge wagons, many pretty villages, and cottages and farms tucked away in gay flower gardens, perfect the rural scene.

There is so much fascination in the hilly streets and narrow alleys that lie below the grey castle of Lewes, that time spent amidst them passes by almost unnoticed. Houses and shops crowd one on another, displaying a wealth of colour and diversified form. Under the trees of the castle precincts, behind the great barbican, is an oasis of peace. On the distant hill of Mount Harry, easily visible from the walls of the keep, Henry III and de Montfort met in conflict in 1264; the scene of the battle can be reached by ascending the prehistoric chalk way that leads over the Downs beyond the church. Northward from Lewes runs the undulating road for East Grinstead, by way of Chailey Common and Sheffield Park. At Dane Hill byways diverge to the left for Horsted Keynes and West Hoathly, situated in the very pleasant forest country of Sussex, once famous for its iron industry. Here East Grinstead is within easy reach. To the west are Worth Forest, Balcombe Forest, and Tilgate Forest; eastwards, lying between Forest Row, Withyham, Wych Cross, and Crowborough, is the exceptionally beautiful district of woods, eminences, heaths, and open moorlands, belonging to Ashdown Forest.

RURAL ESSEX

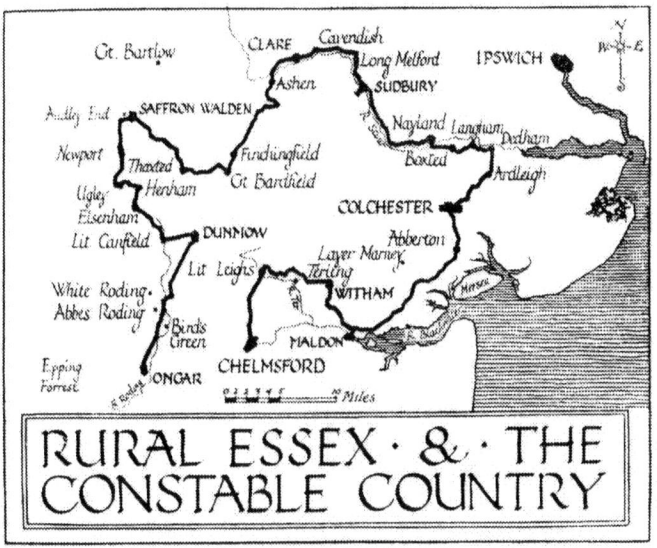

RURAL ESSEX · & · THE CONSTABLE COUNTRY

ROUTE 3

FOR time out of mind the county of Essex has been so maligned, that any support for it as an agreeable touring ground can be advanced only with diffidence. The flats around Tilbury, and Southend at low tide, are certainly not inspiring, but further north there is much natural beauty well worth exploring. In the matter of roads there is little cause for worry, beyond a liability to skid on the Essex clay of the byways in wet weather, and there are few difficult hills.

All who care to make for Ongar, beyond the woodlands and fern of Epping Forest, and then go northwards, will see the woody character of the scene continued up the valley of the River Roding, for at one time these clay lands were covered with forest. There is a good road all the way to Dunmow, and it bisects a tract of country so remote and unsophisticated, so far from railways and as yet untouched by the motor 'bus, it is almost impossible to realize it lies within

thirty miles of London. Here may be seen flattish cultivated
fields, rows of ricks packed closely together, many oak trees,
strong farm horses, field pursuits in summer, and hounds
and riders on crisp November mornings. There are also
quaint old men on antique tricycles, and rustics, picturesquely
clad, who will discourse on their new occupation of sugar-
beet growing. Village blacksmiths yet function in these
parts, and the regular beat of the wood-cutter's axe may be

BRIDGE OVER THE RODING, BIRD'S GREEN.

heard. The kindly custom of passing the time of day, or
giving "good-night" to the stranger, still obtains among
the villagers.

The River Roding, picked out by lines of feathery trees,
winds through a low vale. It gives the principal name of
Roding, or Roothing, to a large number of villages that lie
on, or near, to the Dunmow road. Each is worth a visit,
and in almost every one of these quiet places are old houses of
interest, notably Rookwood Hall, near Abbes Roding, and
Colville Hall and Camoas Hall at White Roding. At
Little Canfield, to the east of Dunmow on the Bishop Stort-

ford road, the right-hand turning winds through Elsenham, Henham, Ugley—quite belying its name—and gains the London highway that leads northward to Newport, a long village remarkable for the quantity and variety of its old domestic buildings. Crown House, close by the roadside, is a particularly graceful example of external parge-work. It is one of the many houses traditionally associated with the fair Nell Gwynn, and even though the date on the porch is five years later than the time of her death, the popular belief must not be questioned! Three miles further on is the great mansion of Audley End (1610), favoured by kings, praised by Evelyn, and thought by Samuel Pepys to be especially good as to its cellar, "where we drank most admirable drink." The house may be well seen from the highway, before returning to the lane which runs by the park, passes near to the old brick almshouses, and ends in Saffron Walden.

The corner of upper Essex in the neighbourhood of Saffron Walden, Thaxted, Great Bardfield and Finchingfield, and up to the ridge of the Cambridgeshire border, is a delightful ground for wandering. Many little hills and shallow valleys ensure a constant change of scene, there are plenty of trees, and the roads and lanes, which wind a good deal, are always pretty. The tranquillity of the scene helps to bring the feeling of being in the very heart of the country, while the traveller passes by little white villages, patches of pasture, and fine corn-lands. As the district lies on the chalk, the old buildings are often of plaster. This material gave scope to local craftsmen, who fashioned it into patterns, and panels, and modelled reliefs. Such work is constantly in evidence, and the house in Church Street, Saffron Walden, formerly the Sun Inn and a headquarters of Cromwell, has notable examples of plaster ornamentation.

Ashen is on the verge of the Stour valley. Onward the river is always near, as the way is made through Clare, past Cavendish church and Long Melford green, and into Sudbury, which, like Clare, is a charming country town full of old timbered and plaster houses. By the north bank of the river the road reaches Nayland, once a wool town, and now, in its old age, an ideal place in which to count the sunny hours, catch perch, or saunter by calm waters. Over the bridge, and by the first turning on the left to Boxted, is the way into haunts that once were trodden by the genial and inspired artist, John Constable. The wide vale that he knew, and many of the things he loved to paint, cannot have greatly changed with the passing of years. The thatched cottages, the mills, the pretty villages, each with a square church tower, and the river winding between green pastures are still to be seen, clumps of trees, too, and lines of willows, and poplars, and elms, that bring a peculiar light contrast of colour to the deeper tones of the wooded undulations that encircle the vale. The narrow lane from Nayland gives views across the

ESSEX FLATS BELOW ABBERTON.

river, with Stoke church—one of Constable's favourite subjects—always high against the skyline. After Boxted and Langham, where a capital mill may be found away down to the left, the Ipswich highway bears down Gun Hill. From this point is an ideal approach to Dedham, embracing all the charms of the Stour valley scenery. The village view makes an impressive group of church and red roofs set amidst the opalescent greenery of the foliage, and surrounded by water-meadows, patches of woodland, and sloping lands. Constable was born in the neighbouring village of East Bergholt—the house has been pulled down—and by the river a mile away from the village are his famous subjects of Flatford Mill and Willy Lott's cottage.

From Dedham the main road up the hill runs to Ardleigh, and enters Colchester by East Hill. This good old market town is one of the most interesting places in the kingdom. Its streets are quite a quarry for the seeker of ancient churches

THE STOUR VALLEY, DEDHAM.

and inns, of doorways with delicate porches, and comfortable bow-windows. There are Roman relics and a castle as well, and the town is rich in memories of Old King Cole, Cymbeline, Boadicea, and the Emperor Claudius. The Mersea road to Abberton, and thence to Maldon, is within reach of the Essex islands and flats, to be seen on Mersea and along the mouth of the Blackwater River. In the opposite direction is the fine brick structure of Layer Marney Tower, belonging to the early sixteenth century. Round by Maldon and Witham, up towards the River Ter near Terling, and as far as Little Leighs, will reveal more attractive country before we gain the highway that leads to Chelmsford.

ROUTE 4

THE beauty of the Thames is both widely known and constant. Along the river's course, where it divides the counties of Buckingham, Berkshire, and Oxford, and on by the Isis to the Cotswolds, there constantly recur memorable scenes of waterway and vale. Grey walls and towers, old churches, villages and country towns, boats, locks, and resorts of youth and pleasure, reflect times past and present.

A little before Egham, on the Exeter Road past Staines, a right-hand turning leads by the river to Runnymede, which, with the neighbouring Magna Charta island, recalls that fight for English liberty made in the year 1215. A short distance beyond, and with the entry into Berkshire, the magnificence of Windsor begins, first heralded by the noble timber that extends away to the Great Park. In quick succession appear the castle towers of the Kings of England, the town below, and old winding streets, picturesque in name and aspect. Castle, town, and park yield enough to beguile many pleasant hours. Windsor as a whole is best seen from the river bridge, or from the meadows. On the Buckinghamshire side of the stream is the great quadrangle of Eton College, surrounded by school buildings and the famous playing fields.

The road through Clewer, following the south side of the river, starts on the left of the main street of Windsor.

PLATE V.

A Lane by the River Roding.

Cottages at Great Bartlow.

The Stour, Nayland.

PLATE VI.

THE THAMES AT HAMBLEDON LOCK.

PRINCES RISBOROUGH.

CLAVERING VILLAGE, ESSEX.

BY THAMES AND CHILTERNS

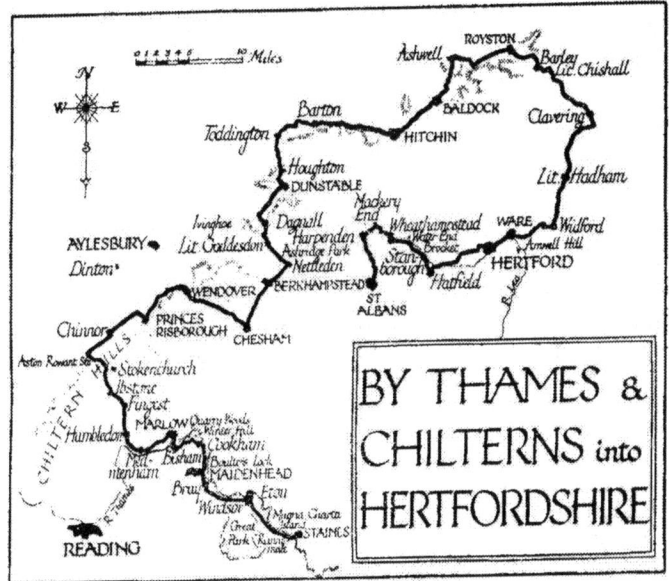

About five miles distant a lane leads to Bray, where lived that opportunist, Simon Aleyn, the vicar of the well-known song. Here, also, is the seventeenth-century Hospital of the Fishmongers Company, superbly pictured by Fred Walker in " The Harbour of Refuge." The way then goes to Maidenhead, where it ends in the Bath Road. Thence, by a right and a left turn, some of the finest Thames scenery may be found—Boulter's Lock, Cliveden Reach and, after passing through Cookham and bearing to the right past the common, the wonderful view from Winter Hill, and the glory of Quarry Woods. These having been seen, and the awkward descent to Bisham and its Abbey accomplished, the way leads over the river into the High Street of the old-world town of Marlow. The turning at the left, by the Crown Hotel, leads to as fair a scene as may be wished for. The broad expanses of the Thames vale extend, west and south, from near hillocks that are partly clothed by groves of beech trees, always beautiful, but finest of all in their sunlit autumn garb of brown and gold. In a little over three miles is Medmenham, of "Hell Fire Club" notoriousness. At Hambledon Lock, not far beyond, all who spend a few moments on the plank-way, behind the mill, will be well rewarded by the views above and below mid-stream.

By proceeding along the right-hand road, for Hambledon village and Fingest, a change of prospect, almost sudden and abrupt, is encountered. The level lands of the Thames are left behind; the outlying hills of the Chilterns dominate the landscape. Although the way up to Fingest follows a valley which, with its fields and elms and old thorns, is green and pleasant to look upon, the greatest attractions are to the right, and the left, and ahead, where smooth rounded contours delicately blend one with another as far as the eye can trace. The chalk of these hills brings a whitish tint to the brown ploughed fields, and the soft warm colour of the grass slopes takes on new qualities with the play of sunshine and shadow and the glow of evening light. Flint walls of churches and cottages, bright and sparkling, provide a harmonious contrast to their natural surroundings. But lovely beyond description are the great woods. Mostly of beech, mixed with fir and larch, they cover many of the long eminences, or extend downwards towards the valleys. Their colouring, especially in October, presents an unforgettable sight.

At Fingest, by turning first left, then right (for Ibstone), a steep little hill, rough of surface, must be mounted. This done, everyone, whether awheel or afoot, must pause to look back to the south; the view is superb. (See Illustration, opposite). Upward again, more hills and woods, Ibstone Green, and then the end of the 700 feet climb at the main Oxford road near Stokenchurch. Round to the left is Aston Hill and another prodigious view—this time over and beyond Oxford and Buckingham. It is but one of the many vast prospects that the northern spurs of the Chilterns command, all the way from the hill above Chinnor to Ivinghoe Beacon.

At the foot of the heights is the Icknield Way, often in the form of a hard road, and sometimes, as at Bledlow, marked by a delightful track. Just beyond Aston Rowant Station

THE CHILTERNS AT FINGEST.

it is encountered and, to the right, can be followed as far as the Great Central Railway, where a right branch leads to Princes Risborough. Here, exposed by the chalk of the hillside, is the Whiteleaf Cross, of very ancient though doubtful origin. On to Wendover and Chesham, through historic Berkhampstead, past the station to Nettleden, and turning left, by Ashridge Park, Little Gaddesden, Dagnal, and Dunstable, runs through more Chiltern country of deep wooded dells, beech groves and bracken, uplands, clear streams, and small pretty towns and villages.

Dunstable stands at the intersection of the Watling Street and the Icknield Way. Through the town, in the driving rain of November 5, 1605, the Gunpowder Plotters wildly rode in their flight up the great North-West Road towards Warwickshire. In the coaching era, too, Dunstable witnessed bustling days, when celebrated coaches halted, and passed on, to set up remarkable records of pace and time for the Holyhead journey. At the end of the main street is a turning for Houghton Regis, Toddington, and a country way, by Barton, to Hitchin, just over the Hertfordshire border. From Hitchin to Baldock and Ashwell—where the rising Cam literally springs from a great hollow beside a splendid Early English church tower—and on through Royston, Barley (of the "Fox and Hounds" inn sign), Little Chishall, Clavering, and the Hadhams, the scenery is always of that thoroughly English character that depends upon much greenery, farms, and villages. It is also a chalk country, shewing many groups of rural buildings, and sometimes a country house, faced and patterned with plaster.

Widford, a few miles ahead, is in the "hearty, homely, loving Hertfordshire" of Charles Lamb. At "Blakesmoor," which used to stand on the old Ware road beside the Ashe stream, he spent many happy days of childhood with his grandmother, Mrs. Field. To the left of the churchyard gate,

"On the green hill-top,
Hard by the house of prayer, a modest roof
And not distinguished from its neighbour barn,
Save by a slender, tapering length of spire.
The grandame sleeps."

By following the course of the stream, first passing near to Blakesware House that has succeeded "Blakesmoor," the little town of Ware is reached. It is full of peeps through archways, and cobbled walks, while summer-houses, built by the townmen of another age, overhang the river. The river is the Lea, that called Piscator and Venator on that "fine, fresh May morning" of the opening lines of *The Compleat*

HERTFORDSHIRE ELMS, WIDFORD.

Angler. Amwell Hill, and the watery scenes to which Isaac Walton has added enchantment and undying beauty, lie a little to the south.

Hertford has many good houses, and much that is picturesque by its castle and river. There are noble park-lands as far as Hatfield, a stretch of the Great North Road to Stanborough, and the big woods of Brocket when the left-hand turning for Wheathampstead is followed. Just over the deep ford at the Ayot Green signpost is Water End, a beautiful gabled farmhouse of the seventeenth century. After turning to the right at the "Swan" in Wheathampstead, crossing the stream, and bearing to the left past the railway bridge, a lane opposite the "Cherry Trees" inn on the Luton road leads, by its first turning to the left, to Mackery End, celebrated in Charles Lamb's most exquisite essay. The farmhouse—modernised since the essayist's days—and the old barns and outbuildings, lie almost on the roadside, quite near to a Jacobean mansion. It is still a calm, sequestered spot, much like it was on that memorable day in June when

THE SUMMER-HOUSES AT WARF.

"the air breathed balmily about it," and the neighbouring scene has little changed since "Elia" was Bridget's "tender charge in those pretty pastoral walks, long ago, about Mackery End, in Hertfordshire." The lane round the mansion, bordered by elms, drops down between open cornfields. At Harpenden the main highway is gained, leading to the great tower of St. Albans Cathedral, rising high over ancient streets and the remains of Roman Verulamium.

DIVISION II

SOUTH-WESTERN ENGLAND

(Shewn on Map, facing Introduction, p. viii)

TERMINATED by the south and west coastline, the Bristol Avon, the Bath Road, the roads connecting Newbury and Southampton, and including the Isle of Wight, this division of England, exceptionally rich in its features, will certainly be the objective, sooner or later, of all tourists on the road. Over it run the great highways to the West—the historic road to Bath, and the equally famous route to Exeter through Andover, Salisbury, Dorchester and Axminster. Hardly less celebrated is the way to the capital of the West by Andover, Amesbury, Wincanton and Ilchester, which was used by the speedy "Telegraph" coach. Nearer to the coast Exeter is gained by a route embracing Romsey, Wimborne and Dorchester. Onward to Land's End the big main road enters Okehampton, Launceston, Bodmin, Redruth and Penzance; here the concluding stages of cyclists' record-making attempts have been witnessed. The well-known Motor Cycling Club's London-Land's End Trial crosses the whole area. In 1926 it came down through Devizes, Shepton Mallet, Taunton, Lynmouth, Bodmin and Perranporth, and included such test hills as Beggars Roost and Bluehills Mine. In a north-easterly direction the Fosse Way strikes upward to Bath from the coast, and other roads, some of them also of great antiquity, take a similar course. Many of these routes going from south to north hold great attractions—in many cases more lanes than roads—and have the character of bank, hedgerow, and wayside interest that comes with age. Particularly fruitful in this wise are the runs in the middle west—that up the Avon valley from Christchurch to

Amesbury and Marlborough, those from Blandford to
Shaftesbury and Warminster, from Dorchester to Yeovil,
Charlton Mackrell and Glastonbury, from Honiton to
Taunton and Dunster, and so forth—embracing stretches of
quiet road, passing clusters of cottages and small towns now
almost forgotten. Byways in Wiltshire, Dorset, and Somerset open up remote country of a kind to be found on Cranborne Chase, in the district of the Thomas Hardy novels, and
throughout the mid-Somerset plain; the beauty of sunken
lanes in Devon and north-west Somerset is proverbial;
moorland roads and tracks can be followed at will on Exmoor,
Dartmoor, and Bodmin Moor; while a length of magnificent
coastline offers boundless possibilities for exploration on
wheel or foot in secluded places where land and sea meet.

In few directions do roads lack hills. Chalk undulations
spreading from Dorset to Salisbury Plain and Marlborough
Downs, the limestone of the Mendips, oolites reaching the
coast at Lyme Bay, a geological formation much diversified
in the neighbourhood of Blackdown Hills, sandstone in the
Quantocks, Devonian rocks and grits, and granite protusions
between Dartmoor and Land's End, account for gradients
in many parts which are often steep, and not infrequently
dangerous, to users of the highways. This district, in
physical aspect multiform, obviously embraces scenes of
great variety. Radiating from Salisbury Plain, the wide
uplands of Wiltshire and Dorset, themselves often capped with
belts of trees, lead to deep vales and the woods of Savernake,
Cranborne Chase, and the New Forest. Across the Solent is
the Isle of Wight, a miniature of verdure, downs and cliffs,
shewing best in its western half which embraces Yarmouth,
Carisbrook, Arreton and Whitwell. The country further
west, rising over Maiden Newton, Yeovil and Crewkerne, and
reaching to considerable eminences in the Blackdown,
Quantock, and Mendip Hills, holds much that is fine to see,
whether it be looked for on tree-clad slopes, or in views
to distant landscapes. The genial southern climate encourages a profusion of wild flowers; primrose banks in Spring
are a source of delight, while pink and white orchard bloom
in the warm valleys and lower lands continues through
villages and towns which seem to belong rather to the past

INTRODUCTION

than the present. Still more to the west, Exmoor and Dartmoor—both places of open wildness and solitude—rise over a belt of Devon intersected by deep winding lanes. Here the villages, brilliantly white in their walls, and snug with deep thatched roofs, are almost hidden in greenery. The banks of the River Tamar, hardly less wonderful than those of the Dart, make part of the boundary of Cornwall, a county remarkable for its coastline and romantic harbours. There are other parts of the coast to see, too; the headlands of north Somerset and Devon, Lyme Bay, Portland Bill, Purbeck Island, Poole Harbour, and the mouth of the Avon at Hengistbury Head, are all notable.

Throughout the south-west district the early days of England are recalled by many objects of antiquity. Travelling by road, one is constantly brought face to face with unfamiliar landmarks. Of themselves they are often neither impressive nor beautiful, hardly to be noticed by the chance observer—a mere disturbance in the earth, a low mound, or an isolated stone. On the other hand, it may be one lights upon Stonehenge looming in the dusk, the gigantic mound of Silbury Hill, Badbury Rings commanding views over Wimborne and The Needles, Maiden Castle, near Dorchester, Cadbury Castle, north of Sherborne, the Longstones on Dartmoor, or one of the cromlechs at Land's End. Such places as these, together with the earthworks and stones which abound in the south-west, can conjure up in the mind vivid pictures of some of the activities of Britain's earliest inhabitants who are almost unknown to history. Here is material in plenty for archæological speculation and fancy; what tourist does not feel this, for instance, on the road from Marlborough to Avebury, or in the high country bordering the River Wylye? Of British trackways, some of the most ancient came out of Salisbury Plain. They followed the ridges of hills to the east and south coasts, or turned northwards, as the Ridge Way still does. This old route, after leaving the tribal boundary ditch known as Wansdyke, crosses the Bath Road between Silbury Hill and Fyfield, thence continuing over Marlborough Downs.

Here are many relics of the long, Roman occupation: the Roman road to Bath, which traces a green way west of the

Devizes coaching highway, curious remains in Bath itself, a remodelled British Fosse Way, the Old Sarum-Bristol Channel route, embracing fine country at Grovely Wood, Great Ridge Wood and on the Mendips, Ackling Dyke, near Cranborne, many fortifications, and signs of domestic life. Glastonbury, Tintagel and Dozmaré Pool, each traditionally associated with the Arthurian Romance, are but three of numerous localities that suggest those legends and beliefs which have ever been prevalent in the west. Nowhere have old customs and observances remained longer ingrained. The power of ecclesiastical influence and the persistence of mediæval tradition are evident alike in names and buildings—in Huish Episcopi or Abbotsbury, in the great cathedrals and magnificent church architecture of Wiltshire, Dorset and Somerset, in the rood screens and pulpits of Devon.

Historical stories in the south-west are some of the most romantic and colourful. They include King Alfred's hiding on Athelney, commemorated by a stone pillar near the village of Boroughbridge, the sighting of the Armada from Plymouth Hoe, deeds of Drake, Raleigh, Hawkins and the Devonshire adventurers in the days of "good Queen Bess," and the landing of William of Orange at Brixham. The web of history in these parts is also woven round events of sinister import, suggested by Wareham, from which Canute ravaged the country, while Lyme, Sedgemoor and Woodlands Park, Cranborne, are associated respectively with the rebel Duke of Monmouth's hopes, defeat, and capture. There, too, is Taunton Castle, inseparably connected with the Bloody Assize of Judge Jeffreys. But one of the greatest appeals of the south-west is to be found in its small towns, villages, and homes that, better than anything else, mirror the old life and ways of the people. In a district mainly agricultural, and little affected by the spread of industrialism, place after place of unusual charm will be seen. The buildings, examples of quiet and homely taste, are always characteristically English, whether they be looked for in such towns as Wareham, Blandford, Amesbury, Devizes, Corsham, Sherborne, Wells, Beaminster, Dunster, Totnes, Dartmouth, Fowey and St. Ives, or in the singularly beautiful manor-houses spread over Wiltshire, Dorset and Somerset, of which Stockton,

South Wraxall, Wool, Clifton Maybank, Lytes Cary and Barrington are but a small proportion. No less attractive are the stone and flint villages in the Avon valley above Salisbury, the white walls and thatch of the New Forest district and Devon, and the simple granite dwellings of Cornwall.

ROUTE 5

THE Bath Road from Reading to Newbury, and on to Hungerford, keeps to the pleasant wide valley that is watered by the River Kennet. Hungerford is a genial little town of warm-toned bricks and tiles, still known, as it was to John Evelyn, for good fat trout and grayling; one may see them, and perhaps catch them, in the stream by the mill and below the bridge. Not far away the lovely glades of Savernake Forest, of quite exceptional beauty and magnitude, extend right to Marlborough, where quiet dignity reigns supreme. To be in Marlborough's great wide street on a sunny summer morning, and to watch the play of light and shade under the columned arcades, meanwhile noting the very Georgian character of the scene, is to feel at once transported right back to the eighteenth century. Then the venerable town's associations come to mind—coaches and post-chaises hurrying on to London or to Bath, and the figures of Fanny Burney and Mrs. Thrale, Walpole, Sheridan, Garrick, and a host of other celebrities making the journey to or from the western spa. Long before them, too, Charles I was in the town soon after the first battle of Newbury, and Samuel Pepys, on June 15, 1668: "lay at the Hart; after paying the reckoning, 14s. 4d. and servants 2s., poor 1s., set out." The architectural features of the street, particularly those expressed in hanging tiles, or in brickwork enlivened by vitrified headers, are well worth seeing.

The country bordering the Bath road, after Fyfield is passed, opens out into the rolling expanses of the downs. There are few houses or trees and the lonely scene is full of evidences of the early inhabitants of Britain. Many barrows, or burial mounds, are plainly visible on the hill-tops; there

are the sarsen stones of the Devil's Den, supposed to be a sepulchral monument. The district is very rich in military earthworks. A right-hand turning, for Avebury, leads to other remarkable signs of an ancient civilization. Around the well-known stones of Avebury, which are computed to have originally numbered 649, controversy has raged for many decades. Although numerous theories have been advanced, their origin and uses have never been proved. So, while authorities differ, it is as relics of a people long since lost in the mists of time that these monuments most impress the onlooker. Within the great earthworks that encircle the stones, and mostly built of broken monoliths, is a pretty village, complete with thatched cottages, an inn, a grey old church, and a rambling manor-house of many gables.

All the way to the south, as far as Salisbury Plain and beyond, the country is remarkable for earthworks. Not far along the Devizes road from Avebury the enormous artificial mound of Silbury Hill is seen on the left. After Beckhampton Green is the trackway of the Roman road to Bath. The earthen wall of Wansdyke next comes into view, winding away over soft green hills. These are followed

EARTHWORKS AND STONES, AVEBURY.

by a sudden rich vale at Bishops Canning, pale mysterious distance ahead, and a drop down to Devizes, a town quite as attractive as Marlborough for old associations, houses and inns, and bedecked in summer with flowers that hang from street lamps and balconies. From the crossroads at Devizes Green the way for Westbury, which bears to the right just short of Lavington Station, often passes between limestone rocks and dense woods, and frequently mounts steepish hills. Potterne, the first village, has a splendid range of

THE SHAFTESBURY ROAD AT SEMLEY.

timbered buildings, once known as the "White Horse" inn. Each village beyond—Great Cheverell, Erlestoke and Edington—is full of charm, and all lie under the outlying hills of Salisbury Plain, to be gained by numerous trackways and paths. A succession of green slopes, woodlands, deep banks overgrown with bracken, and magnificent distant views to the north, make this road into Westbury one of exceptional beauty. Under the hills again, and Warminster's stone-built High Street is reached. Next, by the infant River Wylye, comes Heytesbury, the gateway to a string of pretty waterside villages—Knook, the two Codfords, and on the other side of the stream, Stockton Manor of Elizabethan stone and flint, and Wylye. Over Salisbury Plain, by Winterbourne Stoke, a way leads to Stonehenge, Amesbury's ancient inn, and the rural road by the Avon which passes under the shadow of Old Sarum into Salisbury. These Wiltshire river valleys contain some of the best examples of stone and flint building in England.

There is a wealth of interest, both historical and architectural, around the graceful spire of Salisbury. Three miles away, at Wilton, the route winds along the pretty Nadder vale, passing Clarendon House, Dinton, the gateway and great fifteenth-century barn of the Abbess of Shaftesbury at Tisbury, and the castle ruins of Wardour belonging to the last years of the fourteenth century. The way then goes by common and hill, eventually mounting up to the high-placed town of Shaftesbury. In the sylvan village of East Knoyle, some miles to the north and reached by the turning at Semley Station, a stone panel records " In a house near this spot was born on the 28th October 1631 Sir Christopher Wren — Architect — Mathematician — Patriot—a son of the rector of this parish"; the date, incorrectly given, should be October 20th, 1632. By more hills from Shaftesbury, giving extensive prospects over Blackmoor Vale, the sinuous road leads round Melbury Hill. Continuing southwards to Blandford, it skirts little villages, fine church towers, country houses, and many park-lands sheltered by the slopes of downs.

OLD SHAFTESBURY MILESTONE.

Blandford, in its long main street, shews as good a collection of eighteenth-century buildings as may be found in any country town. The brickwork, almost unspoiled by alteration, is mostly purple and grey in colour, relieved here and there by red, and enriched with string courses and projecting cornices. The hilly Blandford-Dorchester road, which commands fine views over Milton Abbas, should be left at the Kingston-Bere Regis signpost, for this turning points into the heart of Thomas Hardy's Wessex. Bere Regis is the " Kingsbere-sub-Greenhill " of the D'Urbervilles, " a little one-eyed, blinking sort o' place," with, however, a splendid church containing relics of the tombs. " Egdon Heath " of the novels, a place of great solitudes and pine trees, extends almost all the way to Wareham. A few miles west of this town will be seen the original of 'Wellbridge" in Wool Manor and bridge.

Wareham is a convenient point for the exploration of Purbeck Island and the romantic Corfe Castle. Thence, round Poole Harbour to Wimborne Minster, beside the Stour to Christchurch, and up the exquisite Avon Valley to Ringwood, is beautiful scenery that has long been known to artists. Eastward is the New Forest, a home of wild ponies; it is still very secluded and remote among the great trees and purple heaths that lie away from the beaten tracks. Lymington, a quaint old place on the Solent, is on the way to Beaulieu Heath and the famous Beaulieu Abbey, from which point the Forest road continues to Lyndhurst and the great woods beyond Minstead.

ROUTE 6

BATH has charm of a particular kind, rarely found in an English town. Its situation is both unusual and fine. Occupying the banks and very steep slopes of a sweep of the Bristol Avon, the city somewhat resembles a huge amphitheatre, with tiers made of white stone buildings and trees. Beautifully situated though it is, and interesting as are its Roman and mediæval monuments, the singularity of Bath lies in its streets and squares and crescents that were planned and built by the two Woods, father and son, for the reception of eighteenth-century society over which Beau Nash once reigned. On all sides—in Queen Square, The Royal Crescent, North and South Parades, or in Sawclose where Beau Nash lived—almost every house has a history, has played a part; so great a wealth of dignified classic architecture, bound up in life and literature, no other English town can shew.

The London road for Hyde Park Corner follows the river from Bath, enters Wiltshire, mounts Box Hill and, at Pickwick, gives a right-hand turning for Corsham and Bradford-on-Avon, where the river is crossed for Westwood. The return into Somerset is made at Farleigh Hungerford and Norton St. Philip. Southwards, to the left, lies Frome. In this

PLATE VII.

UNDER MELBURY HILL.

THE AVON AT MIDDLE WOODFORD.

SWAN GREEN, NEW FOREST.

PLATE VIII.

WELLS CATHEDRAL

BEER HEAD, SEATON.

SOMERSET

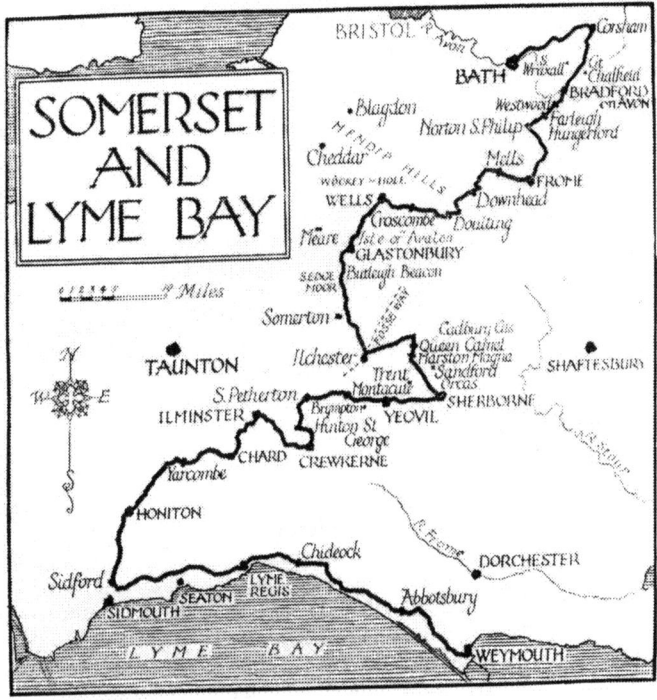

borderland of Wiltshire, as well as throughout Somerset, the story of the country is largely written in stone—in the stone of the churches, manor-houses, and villages. The work of the Somerset masons—a body of craftsmen one of the finest England ever produced—is traceable everywhere, and most notably in the superb church towers. Corsham and Bradford-on-Avon are full of examples, while the manor-houses at South Wraxall, Great Chalfield, and Lower Westwood are exceptional; ruins of the Hungerford's castle, as well as their chapel and tombs, are on the hillside at Farleigh, and in " The George," Norton St. Philip possesses a remarkable mediæval inn that sheltered Monmouth before the battle of Sedgemoor. Here it may be mentioned that the manor-houses, privately owned and therefore not accessible for inspection, may usually be viewed from the churchyards adjoining.

Frome is in hilly country at the end of the Mendips. The hills, and the Somerset plain beyond, together make a tract of country containing great variety in features and aspect. The people are genial and hospitable, old customs survive among them, and this region of legend, which includes the Island of Avalon and Athelney, is the background to the old stories of Joseph of Arimathea and the Holy Thorn, King Alfred and the cakes, and the Arthurian Romance. Except in well-known places like Wells and Cheddar, visitors are not plentiful. Mells, past Frome, with its church, manor and good views, is a characteristic village of these parts. Almost two miles further on, a left-hand turning for Leigh and Downhead leads through the hills, presently dropping down to the famous quarries and tithe-barn of Doulting. From here was derived the material for the building of Glastonbury Abbey and Wells Cathedral. A main road, striking through Shepton Mallet, keeps to the picturesque valley of Croscombe and Dinder. At the end of the jutting rocks of Dulcot Hill the glorious city of Wells appears, dominated by the cathedral and backed in mid-distance by Glastonbury Tor and other pyramidal hills.

Wells is so generally known and very much visited, it is sufficient to state that all those who have not seen it have yet to experience the unique charm of a lovely city that stands, in many respects, as perfect as it did in mediæval days. From Wells, the cavern called Wookey Hole can be visited, and the best of the Mendip scenery, lying between Wookey, Cheddar, and Blagdon. The flat road to Glastonbury is disappointing, and the little town of the Isle of Avalon, round which so much romance and history has centred, has been much spoiled by modern erections. Although the older buildings and ruins lack neither beauty or grandeur, a better impression of Glastonbury is gained from the marsh road to Meare. Stop at one of the dyke-gates, cross the water, and look back. Then will be seen a landscape such as one of the early Italian masters might have taken for the background of a picture of St. Joseph, the flat lands and the softened details of Glastonbury, framed by the sombre lines of the Tor, the Island, and the far-off Mendips, giving a romantic scene fully in tune with the mystery and fame that is gathered there.

The roads from Glastonbury to Sherborne, just over the county border, go through the heart of rural Somerset. First there are wooded hills, curiously shaped, Butleigh Beacon with an obelisk, and views over Sedgemoor. Somerton, charming in its square and old cross, is a little to the right. A climb over Kingsdon Hill leads to Ilchester on the Fosse Way, where a turning on the left, reaching Camel Hill, gives

GREAT CHALFIELD MANOR-HOUSE, WILTSHIRE.

the route into Sherborne through Queen Camel, Marston Magna, and over Rimpton Hill. A traditional site of King Arthur's Camelot on the entrenched hill of Cadbury Castle, the village of Trent, and Sandford Orcas manor-house, are local points of interest. Sherborne is a delightful town, Yeovil is much less attractive, but the road to South Petherton, under the hills that rise south of the mid-Somerset plain, shews the scene, villages and architecture of the West Country at their best. A mediæval manor-house at Preston Plucknett, Brympton Manor, to be seen from the footpath to the church, the magnificent mansion and village of Montacute, Stoke-sub-Hamdon, and the quiet small town of South Petherton, make a chain of sights that should on no account be missed. Yet another exquisite village, Hinton St. George, can be visited on the way to Crewkerne. Undulating to Ilminster—which has a grand church—the route bears south to the hillside town of Chard, through which both Charles I and Monmouth marched, with disaster looming before them. Somerset ends on the good road through the hills to Honiton. The lovely borderland of Devon and the sea lie beyond. From Sidford to Weymouth the coast route, reaching to high elevations by a series of precipitous hills, shews glimpses of coastline and the blue waters of

HINTON ST. GEORGE, SOMERSET.

Lyme Bay; it gives ways down to the shore, and passes through old Lyme Regis, Chideock, Abbotsbury, and fascinating little villages.

ROUTE 7

INSTEAD of following the direct route to Minehead from Taunton, it is better to take the Taunton-Bridgwater road for Kingston and Timbercombe, and there, turning to the left, and the left again, for Cothelstone, gain the Minehead road by a lane on the right some distance past Cothelstone

THE QUANTOCKS

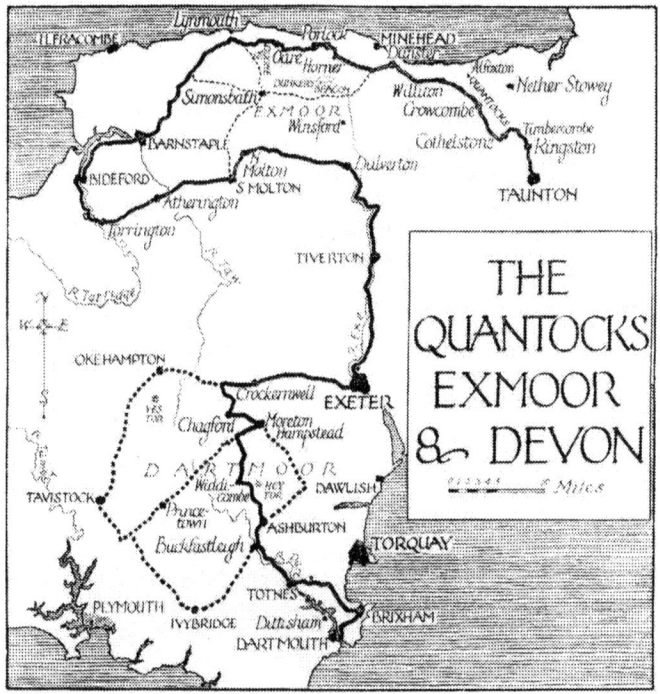

church. By so doing, it is true that such pretty thatched villages as Bishops Lydeard and Combe Florey will be missed, but this alternative route, taking the hills, gives a foretaste of the beautiful scenery of the Quantocks that, stretching away to the gleaming waters of the Bristol Channel, is one long sequence of hanging woods, combes, heaths, barrows, hills and far views, to be seen best of all by walking along the track from Will's Neck to Alfoxton. The road, nevertheless, includes Cothelstone—hill, woods, manor and church—once seen, never to be forgotten, though its history was marred by hangings ordered by the notorious Judge Jeffreys after the battle of Sedgemoor. It was in this lovely country of smooth downs, trees, and brooks, when Coleridge had settled at Nether Stowey, and William and Dorothy Wordsworth were living near by at Alfoxden (ton), that *The Ancient Mariner* and most of the *Lyrical Ballads* first saw the light. But locally the poets were thought to be a curious pair—" C. a crack-brained, talkative fellow; W. either a smuggler or a traitor, and means mischief."

The road goes forward over the hills at Crowcombe to Williton and Dunster, branching away from Minehead for Wootton Courtney, Horner and Porlock. Almost all the villages passed are in some way remarkable; each one is picturesque, while Dunster, crowned by a great castle and neighboured by scenes of more than ordinary delight, is an assemblage of things but rarely met with. Porlock is between the sea and Exmoor. Dunkery Beacon, already seen in the approach from Dunster, rises 1,700 feet over bare and wild, wind-swept wastes. The famous Porlock Hill, a remarkably stiff one to climb, and shewing sea, cliffs, woods, and the distant Welsh coast perfectly blended, gives at its crest a left-hand way, through the northern heights of the Moor, to Oare, the Doone Valley of " girt Jan Ridd," and Devon. Further exploration of Exmoor can be made from its capital, Simonsbath, by four fairly practicable roads or, penetrating into unrelieved wildness, by the rough byways that lead from them. These moorland routes, be it noted, have difficult gradients, dangerous corners, and bends, all calling for care on the part of motorists and cyclists.

The Barnstaple road is joined a mile to the south of the coast where Lynton and Lynmouth face the strand from a background of towering headlands. By more severe hills, succeeded by flatter lands, Barnstaple and Bideford are reached. Each town has a bridge of many arches, and both of them nurtured adventurous, seafaring men who scoured the seas, or fought the Spanish Armada. Crossing Bideford Bridge, the Torridge is followed to Wear Gifford. Mounting again at Torrington, the expansive country of Devon is viewed, as hill upon hill continues to Atherington (here is a perfect rood-screen in the church), South Molton, North Molton, and along the moorland road to Dulverton. To the north, under a ridge in the valley of the Exe, is Winsford, one of the prettiest of villages; to the south are

DEVON

Exeter and Dartmoor, approached by a fine stretch of highway that is always near shady woods and the river.

Exeter, standing proudly on a site overlooking the Exe, is a worthy capital of the county which shews the perfection of English beauty, perhaps, best of all. The history of the west is bound up in the city. Its cathedral, so fine within,

HORNER VALE, NEAR PORLOCK, EXMOOR BORDER.

is environed by a Close rich in buildings of stone and brick, with here and there a cobbled court shewing through a deep archway. The streets behind, winding and packed close together, are full of charm. Old inns bring to mind the coaching days, when the expeditious "Telegraph" completed the summer journey from the west to Hyde Park Corner between early morning and dusk, while modern adventurers of the road, who brave the Motor Cycling Club's winter run, will gratefully remember High Street and breakfast. The castle mound is a place for bird's-eye views, and from banks of the old canal the city may be seen rising over elm trees. Along the estuary, and close to the coast from Dawlish to Torquay, the country is intersected by those lanes that peculiarly belong to Devonshire—narrow, hedges of irregular height on either side, floral loveliness in the banks, blue sky above, and a strip of sea shewing where the track dips down.

The hilly main road, for Okehampton and Cornwall, steadily ascends up to Crockernwell and the edge of Dartmoor. This great moor of Devon, a home of rare birds, is a high plateau of wildernesses, bogs and glens, most striking in its granite tors that rise high up in curious, fantastic shapes. These enormous rocks, looking above all like the castles and unearthly monsters of fairy tales, have long given rise to local beliefs in the supernatural; to them belong stories of elves and pixies, and a ghostly pack of hounds that hunts by night. Though the scene is wild and rude, it gives every shade of effect under changing climatic conditions—aërial brightness with clear skies, and deep, sombre tones when clouds gather. Dartmoor can be encircled by roads connecting Okehampton, Tavistock, Ivybridge, Ashburton and Moreton Hampstead, while it can be crossed by the Princetown route. On all these ways there is plenty of hill-climbing. Only by the lanes, however, can the real exploration of the Moor be accomplished. Leading from the roads, they take to the heights and usually end at nowhere in particular. Beyond, the inner fastnesses of the Moor are to be explored only on foot. One word of warning is necessary. The mists, which sometimes hang over the Moor for days together, are liable to come down very suddenly, completely obscuring the landscape; violent storms develop rapidly even in summer; and a large-scale map is essential.

At the cross-roads four miles beyond Crockernwell is the turning for Moreton Hampstead, giving a right branch in and out of Chagford, picturesque in its "Three Crowns" inn. Widdicombe lies to the left of the Princetown road, past Moreton, at the foot of Hameldown. It shews a majestic church tower, and also a sign depicting "Old Uncle Tom

WINSFORD, EXMOOR.

Cobleigh and all," figures of the jolly song called "Widdicombe Fair." Next, with the approach to Ashburton, the giant rock of Hay Tor, worth climbing for the panoramas it gives, rises on the left, to be followed by some of the grandest of river scenery in the valley of the Dart near Buckfastleigh and Totnes. The old town of Totnes, famed long ago for its cloth, winds up a hillside. Wonderfully impressive in situation, it charms by its houses of projecting gables with walks underneath. In the church are examples of the canopied screens and stone pulpits for which the county of Devon is notable; others will be found lower down the river at Dittisham and Dartmouth. Over the hills once more—perchance first turning for Berry Pomeroy Castle—and Brixham is gained. This port, the headquarters of the Devonshire fishery, is full of pictures by the quay-side—gleaming fish, stalwart damsels, weathered fishermen, and trawlers moored in the harbour. One long rise and descent, superb views down to the Dart, and then will be seen the ferry waiting to carry the tourist from Kingswear to Dartmouth.

ROUTE 8

PICTURE a county long and nowhere very wide, a coastline beautifully broken by estuaries, bays, and rocky headlands, changeless and wild inland moors, cromlechs and stone circles so old, their origin and history are unknown. Add to these a native people marked by independence and character, superstitious beliefs that still play a part in daily life, folklore and stories of smuggling, shipwrecks, and great bravery at sea, and then one gleans an impression of the meaning of Cornwall. Here, most noticeably, natural environment has played on human consciousness; the place and the people are not to be considered singly, for the two are inseparable. The soul of the Cornish race, the strange traditions, the usages that link up for antiquity with the present, are only to be known—and then but dimly—by those travellers intimately acquainted with this most westerly part of England. But now and again, especially with the peasants in the moorland districts, the chance tourist may observe in a story or action a sudden suggestion of things quite outside the ken of ordinary, everyday experience. And the country itself, though its ways are arduous, is open for all to see.

Cornwall shews best on the coastline and in the small fishing places. No touring route can be made to include the innumerable points where the juxtaposition of sea, coast, bays and hills, together with the presence of boats and shipping, invariably result in the picturesque. Those who make their own directions, using a reliable map and not keeping to a rigid itinerary, will profit most. Avoiding the

PLATE IX.

SEVEN WELLS COMBE, THE QUANTOCKS.

CHAGFORD AND THE DARTMOOR FOOTHILLS

PLATE X.

Cornish Headlands, from Black Head.

Tintagel.

Pentewan Valley, St. Austell.

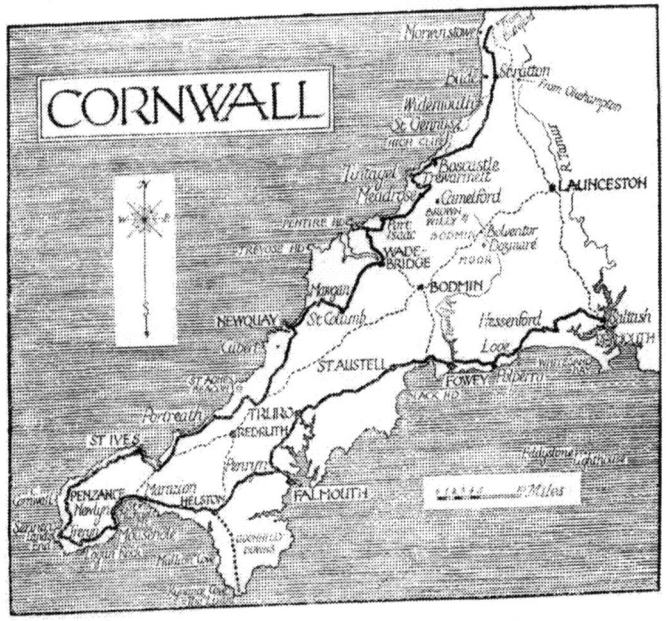

holiday resorts, dropping down to the coast by any usable way that fancy dictates, or following the byways near the sea, such wise tourists will come upon delicious little harbours, villages and fisher-folk, and cottages piled one over another between great clefts in the rocks; sometimes a broad, blue bay opens out, while everywhere will be seen the grandeur of headlands. The narrowness of the county makes it always possible to cross from the bleaker northern side to the more verdant south. Throughout its centre Cornwall is served by the road passing from the glorious River Tamar and fine, old Launceston into the wildness of Bodmin Moor, relieved only by stone walls and miles of heather; beyond Bolventor, midway between high Brown Willy and haunted Dozmaré Pool, this middle route reaches Bodmin, barren country, and the unsightly tin-mining area of Redruth, where two branches go to The Lizard and Land's

End. Both coast and inland roads are notoriously hilly everywhere. Motorists and cyclists require first-class brakes, and great caution in driving is necessary, particularly when the hard roads are left.

Coming out of Devon from Dartmoor and Okehampton, or down from Bideford, the Cornish coast is approached in the parish of Morwinstow. The tiny village is reached by a mile of narrow road. A square church tower on a steep hillside marks the place of Robert Hawker's labours, standing in the midst of scenes bound up with the old life he vividly pictured. At the end of the valley is the sea, breaking on those rocks that have claimed many a gallant ship. To the strand belong exciting adventures, not unconnected with contraband and revenue men. On either side, rising to great heights, are the cliffs from which smugglers and gatherers of wreckage often watched. It is thus worth while turning into Morwinstow, and winding up to its church, for a first impression of Cornwall; ascend Hennacliff, look across Bude Bay to Pentire Point, and the glory of the coastal scene is revealed.

Bude, a mile off the route running due south, is taking to itself the aspect of a resort, but Stratton, a charming old town, still browses on days of Sir Bevil Grenvile and gigantic Anthony Payne, who performed valiant deeds against the Roundheads on Stamford Hill. The main road goes somewhat inland for Boscastle; it gives lanes to the sea and a byway, turning right at the Bude River two miles past Stratton, to grand coast scenery at Widemouth, St. Gennys, Crackington Cove and High Cliff. Steeply dropping into Boscastle, up and down to Tintagel, a turn for Tregatta and Trewarmett, and a bend round, away from Camelford, for Meadrose, Port Isaac and Pentire Head takes one near to things unequalled perhaps even in Cornwall—wild beauty of coast, harbours at Boscastle and Port Isaac, and Tintagel's Rocky Valley and castle of King Arthur. St. Columb Major is beyond Wadebridge. In the wooded valley to the right stand the manor-house of Lanherne and the pretty village of Mawgan. By more fine stretches of coast Newquay is gained, whence an inland route, never far from the sea, touches the coast again at Portreath, first passing within sight

CORNWALL

of Cubert's high spire and St. Agnes Beacon. When St. Ives Bay has been encircled, the quaint old town will appeal by its cobbled streets twisting between quite extraordinary alleys and stairways that lead to homes of fishermen. One more length of road and the rocks of Land's End are approached.

East of Sennen, the little town of Land's End, the entire southern seaboard of Cornwall juts into the waters of the English Channel by a series of projections which give every shade of effect through their curious, broken shapes. The road through Treryn first nears the splintered granite rocks of Logan; passing by the "Merry Maidens," whose nineteen poor bodies were turned to stone for dancing on the Sabbath, it next goes through Mousehole—a nest of ships—to Newlyn and Penzance. Here Mounts Bay traces a fanciful bend round St. Michael's Mount, an exquisite scene on soft, bright days when gleamy light plays on the towers and turrets of the island castle, and nowise suggesting the morning of terror that witnessed, in 1595,

A STREET IN ST. IVES.

the arrival of hostile Spaniards, who burned every house, save one, in Mousehole. Flat to Marazion, the route mounts over hills to Helston. Away to the south, beyond the dreary Downs of Goonhilly, the Lizard pushes out seawards; from its western promontory a pathway follows

POLPERRO.

cliffs, lovely with wild flowers, to the precipitous rocks of Kynance and Mullion Coves. A hilly road leads from Helston to Penryn, where a level way branches to the right for Falmouth. Truro, next reached, is notable for a modern cathedral, designed by Pearson, which groups well when seen from the river of the old city.

A good stretch of undulating highway continues through St. Austell, giving two miles past the town a right-hand turning round Par Sands to Fowey. Between the estuary of the Fowey River and that of the River Tamar, the coast sweeps round in a line of headlands and rocks, turning inland at Looe Island for the bend of Whitesand Bay. Out in the open sea is the Eddystone Lighthouse. On land, deep in valleys that drop straight down to the shore, are fishing places such as Polperro and Looe, and the port of Fowey. This coastline, pleasant when skies are blue and waters are calm, is entirely transformed in times of storm; then it becomes a scene of human anxiety and terror, as people watch the boats battling to reach the harbours. Those who man the boats, and to whom the perils of the deep are part of the daily round, have descended from a long line of sailors from which some of the greatest sea traditions have developed. Fowey, Polperro, East Looe—who shall say which is the most picturesque? Each has a deep, narrow situation, winding streets, alleys, and the quaintest of houses. And all, of course, have memories of smuggling, and annals of reckless deeds committed against foreigners. For Polperro and Looe, from Fowey, the Bodinnick Ferry must be crossed at the "Railway Hotel." Thence great hills lead up and down to the two objectives. The Plymouth road from Looe mounts up for Hessenford. Two miles from this point, by turning left for Liskeard and right at Trerule Foot, Saltash Ferry and the indented banks of the River Tamar are reached.

DIVISION III

MIDLAND ENGLAND

(Shewn on Map, facing Introduction, p. viii)

CENTRED near the very heart of England, this large district has for its eastern boundary a line taken from Newbury to St. Neots, which is continued up to the Humber by the Great North Road. To the south, the Bath Road and the Bristol Avon form the limits, while the western border is made by the frontier of Wales and the coasts of Cheshire and Lancashire. Northwards, the area is terminated by a line connecting Preston and the Humber. Main highways, having their origin in London, cross the Midlands in north, northwest, and westerly directions, thus giving through communications to Yorkshire, Lancashire, and the borderland of Wales. A great number of other good roads, connecting many towns, make the region one of easy accessibility. It includes almost every type of road and byway, ranging from those of the Central and Cheshire Plains to the undulations of Leicestershire, Northamptonshire, the Cotswolds, the Berkshire Downs, and on to the mountainous roads of the Welsh border and the southern Pennines. The particular beauty of some of the ridge-ways calls for special mention—the Wenlock Edge, and those heights overlooking the Vale of the White Horse, the Severn Valley, the Welsh Marches, and the Derbyshire Dales, are fine examples.

So wide an area as that of the Midlands naturally includes diverse geology and varied scenery. The Cotswold Hills, and their continuant uplands in Northamptonshire and Rutland, are made up of the great belt of oolitic limestone and lias that extends without break from Bath to Grantham. Here are villages built of stone, lying in wooded valleys. The heights above them are often bleak and bare, but where

INTRODUCTION 55

the hills drop down to neighbouring vales, trees and vegetation thrive. At these points memorable panoramic views are to be seen, such as the one over the Severn towards the Forest of Dean, the Vale of Evesham from Broadway Tower, Leamington from Edge Hill, and the Northamptonshire scene from the road above Brockhall. Southward rise the chalk downs of Berkshire and Wiltshire—open spaces of springy turf dominated by White Horse Hill. To the west is the old red sandstone of Monmouthshire, Herefordshire, and Shropshire, through which the Usk, the Monnow, the Wye, and the Teme make their sinuous ways between deep, tree-girt ravines. The isolated formations of the Malvern Hills and the Wrekin provide notable view-points, and peculiar local geology accounts for the great rocks of Charnwood, and the bold scenery about Church Stretton and Ludlow. The new red sandstone of the Central Plain and of the flat lands of Cheshire and Nottinghamshire, is interrupted in places by coal measures, sources of supply for the large mining and manufacturing districts of the Black Country, north Warwickshire, and the Potteries. These, together with the busy parts of South Lancashire and Yorkshire, will not attract the tourist. In their vicinity, however, nature still provides compensation for the dullness that man has spread over the landscape. Round about the Peak, where the Pennine Range comes down from the north, much that is impressive and grand may be seen among the moors and the limestone heights; streams flowing rapidly water the dales, and their remarkable character is well shown by the Manifold, the Dove, the Wye, and the Derwent. Where the land falls to the plains, wide stretches of pastoral country bearing plenty of timber occupy the region that once was covered with the old Midland forests, now remembered by the names of Sherwood, Charnwood, Needwood, Arden, Wyre, and Delamere. Not the least beautiful parts of the Midlands border the rivers Severn and Avon; throughout their valleys, and also between the adjacent hopfields of Herefordshire, oaks and elms, lines of willows, orchards, broad green meadows, and villages of unusual attractions, make a continuous chain of prospects always pleasing to the sight.

This inland country has been crossed in all directions by earlier occupants of England, who were sometimes bent on war and sometimes concerned with more peaceful pursuits. Their camps and earthworks are especially evident along the Cotswolds, on the hills throughout the Welsh borders, and among the Derbyshire heights. The Romans, as elsewhere, were busy here, making communications, or building towns. Between Cirencester and Chester, and from Silchester to Doncaster, many signs of their times remain. Some of the fine roads they made are still in daily use, notably the Watling Street, running diagonally from Fenny Stratford to the important ruins of Uriconium at Wroxeter, the Fosse Way connecting Cirencester with Newark, and the street, yet surviving in its original form at Sutton Park near Birmingham, that extends from Derby to Alcester, and away to the south over the Avon at Bidford Bridge. Offa, ruler of the Midland Kingdom of Mercia, is recalled by the names of Offchurch near Leamington, Offenham near Evesham, and by Offa's Dyke, which shews finely on the hills behind Bishops Castle and Clun. The Danes are remembered by such names as Brooksby and Frisby in Leicestershire, and Alfred the Great, who fought them on the Berkshire Downs, was born at Wantage. Onward from William the Conqueror's reign, internal war brought a full quota of trouble to this district. Military castles are many—Oxford, Warwick, Kenilworth, Tamworth, Ashby, Newark, and the strongholds of the Welsh Marches, being among their number—and Evesham, Mortimer's Cross, Bosworth Field, Edge Hill, and Naseby, are but a few of the sites of battles.

The rolling hills of the Cotswolds bring to mind peaceful pages of history, when Cotswold sheep, and wool merchants, were laying the foundations of England's wealth. The Avon valley is for all time associated with Shakespeare's name, and the Washingtons, natives of Northamptonshire, will never be forgotten.

In addition to the glories of a number of cathedrals, the charm of the colleges of Oxford, and the magnificent churches that tell of munificence and prosperous days, there are numerous splendid old towns. The large ones of Gloucester, Hereford, Worcester, Banbury, Warwick, Coventry, Shrewsbury, and Chester, and the smaller towns of Cirencester, Burford, Chipping Campden, Abingdon, Brackley, Ross, Hay, Leominster, Ledbury, Ludlow, Bridgnorth, Tewkesbury, Pershore, Stratford, Oakham, Ashbourne, Bakewell, and Nantwich, as well as a number of others, are full of buildings associated with ancient traditions. Away in the country stand the old mansions and manors for which the Midlands are famous—Owlpen, Compton Winyates, Birts Morton, Ragdale, Stokesay, Pitchford, Old Moreton, Haddon, and a host of others. Some appear from backgrounds of hills and woodlands; others lie below smooth downs, in rich valleys, or between level stretches of greenery. Where the natural products are stone and chalk, they are built of the local materials, while in the old forest regions they are mostly framed in oak. Although the Cotswold villages, with their steep roofs of stone slates and walls of mellow stone, are very lovely, those in the Vale of the White Horse, of quite another type, are almost as fair. To the north, in Derbyshire, the rural stone dwellings shew a sober character, which is in direct contrast to the gay patterning of the black-and-white villages of Cheshire. Set amongst the leafiness of Warwickshire, Worcestershire, Herefordshire, and Shropshire, the timbered cottages, generally roofed with thatch and surrounded by trim gardens, are the very picture of homely, rustic beauty.

ROUTE 9

THE uplands of Northamptonshire, and the Cotswold Hills, are outcrops of the oolitic and lias formations that extend across England from the south coast to Yorkshire. Within the belt of these hills, wide stretches of elevated country, bleak in places and divided into fields by stone walls, are broken by countless wooded valleys through which clear streams flow. High on the slopes, or nestling below them, stand the churches, houses, cottages, and farms, built of the local limestone, that are ever a source of wonder and delight. From some of the ridges, notably those of the Cotswolds, very fine prospects are visible.

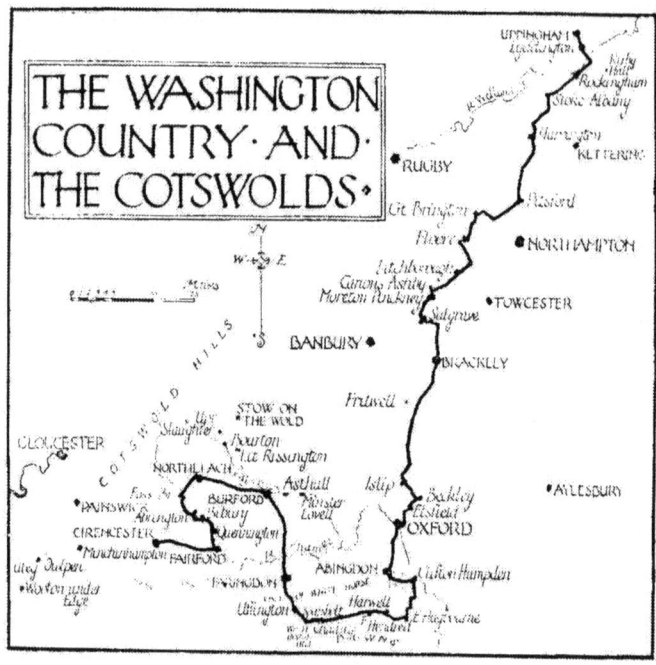

The little town of Uppingham in Rutland, noted for its public school, is on the borderland of the wide valley of the River Welland. The beautiful Bede House of Lyddington is quite near; it belongs to the time of Henry VII, and was once a country seat of the Bishops of Lincoln. On the side of the river south of Caldecott rise the rounded hills of Northamptonshire, leafy and green with the remnants of the old Forest of Rockingham. Many a pleasant hour may be spent, moving from village to village, between Barrowden and Stoke Albany. Mullioned windows and stone doorways, covered with lichens and overhung with creepers, together with trees, parks, and blue distances beyond, add value to the landscape. There is also the great ruined Elizabethan hall of Kirby, close to the steep, irregular byways of Gretton.

THE WASHINGTON COUNTRY

At the top of Rockingham, the Market Harborough road bears round the castle for Stoke Albany. To the left, across the Kettering road and through Harrington, the Northampton highway makes a line to Pitsford, where a right turning goes by the railway station to the Rugby road and Althorpe Park. Leftwards, round the park, is Great Brington. A little to the east, the march of Queen Eleanor's funeral procession from Harby, near Lincoln, to Charing Cross, is commemorated by the lofty and delicate stonework of the crosses at Geddington and Northampton.

To Little Brington came Laurence Washington, after the family home at Sulgrave had been sold. Here he brought up his large family, and here he died in 1616. In the chancel of the hillside church of Great Brington his tomb may be seen. Above the inscription is the Washington coat-of-arms, shewing the stars and bars that are popularly supposed to have given the basis for the United States flag. Laurence's sons prospered in the reign of Charles I,

LAURENCE WASHINGTON'S TOMB, GREAT BRINGTON.

but loyalty to their King eventually brought misfortune. Two grandsons left their troubled native country to seek their fortunes in the New World. John, the elder, settled in Virginia about 1658, and from him was descended the illustrious George. The Washington house at Brington, by no means so well known as Sulgrave Manor, is on the village roadside—a simple stone dwelling, looking much as it did in those far-off Washington days.

Sulgrave can be reached by a pretty way down through the hills to Floore, by a short stretch of the Towcester road, and by a right-hand turning through Litchborough, Canons Ashby, and Morton Pinkney. The home of the Drydens at Canons Ashby, which the poet knew—very old, and picturesque in its Renaissance additions—the church opposite, and the typical Northamptonshire village of Morton Pinkney, especially call for a halt. All good Americans go to Sulgrave

Manor, nowadays very well cared for, and Britishers know it too. But it is always worth a visit. The route is then continued past Helmdon station, through the really charming street of Brackley, and towards Oxford by a gradual descent, leaving haunted Fritwell on the right. A branch to the left, for Islip, ends in a climb up to the secluded Noke-Wood Eaton country, giving wonderful views over Oxford from the wood near Beckley. The entry into the city is made

THE WASHINGTON HOUSE, LITTLE BRINGTON.

through Elsfield, and over Magdalen Bridge. The incomparable " High " lies beyond.

St. Aldates Street to the left of Carfax at the end of Oxford High Street, leads past Christ Church College to Abingdon, one of the very best of the Thames towns, lying snug by the river-side. Abingdon, so lovely in itself, is the gateway to the tranquil Berkshire villages.

Cross the river by the 400-year-old bridge—here pausing to look back at the last and best glimpse of the town—turn to the right over the Thames at Clifton Hampden, and wind through lanes to East Hagbourne, Harwell, East and West

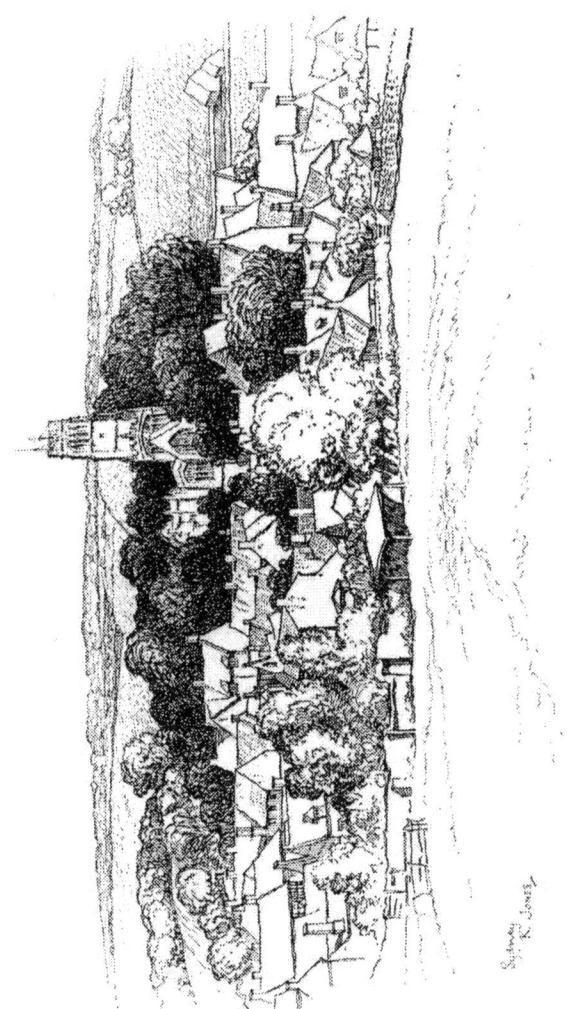

A COTSWOLD WOOL TOWN, NORTHLEACH.

Hendred, Childrey and Sparsholt. In this progression one sees some of the choicest of villages, with shapely plaster houses, oakwork and thatch, bright flower gardens, and spreading trees, looking like little cameos touched in with soft colours. The broad Berkshire downs are always near. Trackways lead up to their grassy crests. There the turf springs to the tread, and earthworks and stones, burial-places of ancient heroes, and signs of pagan rites, give an impression of antiquity.

From the foot of White Horse Hill to Uffington—redolent of scenes connected with Tom Brown's School Days—across the Vale to Faringdon, and up to Burford, means a gradual penetration into the heart of the Cotswold country that William Morris knew so well when he made his home at Kelmscott. Burford, Northleach, Fairford and Cirencester, together with the villages and manor-houses that lie in between them, are some of the wonderful places that lie among the folds of the Cotswold Hills. Centuries ago, when these stretches of upland were one vast sheep-walk, the fame of Cotswold wool was known far and wide. Foreign merchants eagerly sought the fleeces, and pack-horses, following the ancient chalk tracks, carried them to the South Coast ports. This trade in wool, and the manufacture of cloth that subsequently developed, brought much prosperity. Merchants and clothmen acquired great wealth, and some of the houses in which they lived can yet be seen. By their piety and generosity magnificent churches were erected; still they stand as monuments to their founders in spacious times when grace had a place in the daily round. In each of the four towns above mentioned, the churches bear witness to the munificence that went hand in hand with commercial prosperity.

The Cotswold scene, which forms the background to the towns and villages, is made up of high-lying plains and smooth hills. It is enriched by river valleys, such as those of the Windrush and the Coln, and rippling waters harbour fine trout. When the may-fly is up, fishermen's hopes run high; in winter, the notes of the hunter's horn resound over hill and dale. Nowhere in England has a finer style of domestic building been developed. The " grey towns," and

PLATE XI.

BARROWDEN, RUTLAND.

EAST HAGBOURNE, BERKSHIRE.

THE WINDRUSH, MINSTER LOVELL.

PLATE XII.

CRADLEY, UNDER THE MALVERNS.

TINTERN ABBEY.

villages, fashioned of the local limestone, have a character all their own. Every place is full of things to be remembered —Burford, Asthall Manor, Minster Lovel, the villages just off the Northleach highway; and away to the north, Upper and Lower Slaughter, Bourton-on-the-Water, and the Rissingtons. From Fosse Bridge, below Northleach, a beautiful riverside way goes down by Ablington Manor— where Arthur Gibbs penned " A Cotswold Village "—to Bibury, Quennington and Fairford. Two picturesque inns at Fairford, its famous church rebuilt by that prince of wool-merchants, John Tame, and the retired village of Ampney Crucis, will all be seen before entering Cirencester. Standing at the junction of Roman roads, Cirencester has always been a place of importance. Its buildings denote olden prosperity; on market days the busy crowds of farmers tell of present activity. This town is a good centre for further exploration. Away to the west, among the high hills that overlook the Severn Valley, the distant views are of extraordinary magnitude. It is a region of Roman camps, Uley Bury being one of the finest. Other grey towns will be found at Painswick, Minchinhampton and Wootton-under-Edge. Hilly roads lead to many pretty villages, and old gabled houses, like Owlpen, are numerous. Every road has its beauties, constantly changing as each valley is traversed and each ascent is gained.

ROUTE 10

THE River Avon, entering the county of Warwick under the Watling Street near Rugby, makes a devious course through the centre of England until its waters join those of the Severn at Tewkesbury. This river of verdant scenes, winding beneath green banks through an expansive, fertile vale, sweeps round slopes of meadow and cultivated land, rich in orchards and parks. It flows through country towns, and passes by numerous villages of great beauty. The Stratford district embraces the landscape "from which Shakespeare must have derived his earliest ideas of rural

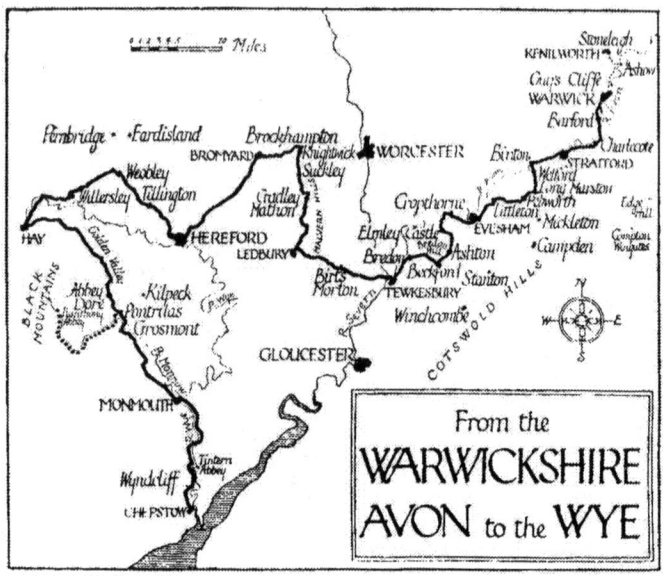

From the WARWICKSHIRE AVON to the WYE

imagery." Lower down the stream, where the current traces fanciful curves under Bredon Hill, is the fine green country of Worcestershire.

Much fame and an influx of visitors, have hardly lessened the attractiveness of the Shakespeare Country. Warwick, for instance, on an ordinary day is just the same delightful town it ever was. It speaks of the glories of the past. There is little hurry in the streets. The morning sun throws narrow Mill Street into shade, and brightens the stonework of the great castle that rises sheer from the river; it brings out the Gothic delicacy of the Beauchamp Chapel, and touches with light the line of High Street between Leicester's Hospital and East Gate. While the familiar view of the castle and river from the Banbury Road is always worth seeing, that from Bridge End, just below the bridge, is hardly less charming. Kenilworth, apart from its magnificent castle ruins, has certainly suffered from too much popularity,

STRATFORD-ON-AVON

but the Avon villages of Ashow, Stoneleigh, and Bubbenhall, Guy's Cliff Mill, Stoneleigh Deer Park, and the watered meadows lying between, are all places for lovers of English scenes.

Two ways lead to Stratford from Warwick West Gate. The more interesting and level road, the lower one, follows the course of the river. It crosses the Avon at Barford, passes to the left of Wasperton, bears to the right round the fine mid-sixteenth century mansion of the Lucys of Charlecote, standing in the deer park that credulous people think was the scene of Shakespeare's poaching adventure, and reaches Clopton Bridge, by the route of Washington Irving's pedestrian visit, so delicately pictured in his memorable sketch "Stratford-on-Avon." Guide-books galore are provided for all who know not Stratford. If the Shakespearean attractions of the town become overpowering through too much emphasis, the wanderer may turn to the beautiful buildings, the picturesque inns, the modern restorations that have brought to light a number of timbered façades, and the riverside walk from the mill by the church. Further afield, some miles to the south-east, is Edge Hill. Its summit, splendid for distant views, is gained by the well-known ascent up to Sunrising, a house in which Charles I breakfasted on the morning of the Edge Hill fight. In a wooded valley at the foot of the hills beyond Tysoe, so hemmed in

HARVARD HOUSE,
STRATFORD-ON-AVON.

with greenery that it is difficult to find, is that lovely Tudor building, Compton Winyates.

The Evesham road from Stratford, mounting up Bordon Hill, drops down to the Avon at Binton Bridge. North and south of the river are the eight villages known as the Shakespeare villages which tradition has associated with further misdeeds of our national bard. His morning thoughts, after night labours with beer, are supposed to have framed the popular lines on Pebworth, Marston, Hillborough, Grafton, Exhall, Wixford, Broom, and Bidford. Over Binton Bridge leads to Welford—still charming in spite of new houses—and on to Long Marston, where a right-hand turning goes through Pebworth and the Littletons to the gardens and plum trees of the Evesham Vale. A stop should be made at Middle Littleton to see the fine group formed by the church, tithe-barn and manor-house.

Evesham and Tewkesbury are good old towns owning certain things in common. Each was the scene of a final battle that brought to a close a period of internal war. In one the relics of a great abbey remain; in the other is a grand abbey church. Both towns are watered by the river Avon, and although Evesham is the busier, its timbered houses and interesting streets compare with those of Tewkesbury. The tract of country that divides them, celebrated among artists as a sketching ground, shews rich passages of landscape at every turn. Numberless cottages suggest rustic scenes, and every village gives a picture. It is a region of high elm trees, and they crowd the vale below the gentle slopes of Bredon Hill. If the season be spring, billowy masses of plum blossom will be seen transforming the orchards into seas of shimmering white. In the distance, a few miles away, the soft lines of the Cotswold Hills enclose many a little masterpiece of stone architecture in such places as Mickleton, Chipping Campden, Broadway, Stanton and Winchcombe. The way through this delicious country goes from Evesham Bridge by the road on the side of the river opposite the Bell Tower. At Little Hampton the Pershore road is followed for Cropthorne. Beyond this village, lanes to the left reveal the Bredon Vale villages of Bricklehampton, Elmley Castle, Ashton, Beckford and

Overbury. At the village of Bredon the Tewkesbury highway is gained.

The rich landscape continues from Tewkesbury to Ledbury, and across Herefordshire to Hay. The Malverns make the Worcestershire boundary; away to the west is the high borderland of Wales. At Hollybush, short of Ledbury, and not far from the moated house of Birts Morton, hilly roads are encountered. Past Ledbury (where no one should miss seeing Church Lane and the Market Hall) they wind below the Malverns, through the pretty villages of Mathon

THE VALE OF EVESHAM AND BREDON HILL.

and Cradley to Stifford Bridge. After the stream has been crossed by a left turn, a way branches to the right for Suckley, Knightwick, and the formidable Bromyard highway. In a hollow down to the right, surrounded by a moat, and approached by a gatehouse, stands Lower Brockhampton Manor, a gem of the fourteenth century.

Bromyard to Hereford means a drop down over several stiffish bumps to the rivers Lugg and Wye, with good distant views over orchards and hopfields. At White Cross, on the Hereford-Kington road, the turning to the right gives, at the fork beyond the railway, a left-hand route through wooded hillside scenery to Tillington, and the remarkable black-and-white town of Weobley. Pembridge and Eardisland, both full of timberwork, are quite near. A splendid road through

Willersley eventually reaches Clifford Castle and Hay, where the Wye comes down from Wales. This Herefordshire country, the district of John Abel, the seventeenth-century carpenter-architect, is especially notable for its half-timber buildings, representing a phase of architecture that gradually developed through the efforts of local craftsmen, who handed traditions of workmanship down from father to son. In towns and villages, and among meadows and trees, the bright patterns of the black-and-white dwellings, barns and pigeon-houses are constantly seen.

There are such vast charming prospects between Hay and the mouth of the Severn, that the traveller will be pleased with almost any road he cares to follow. The Golden Valley route, as its name implies, will not disappoint. It includes Abbey Dore, beautiful in its stonework, and makes possible short detours to Llanthony Abbey and the Norman church at Kilpeck. Llanthony Abbey lies in a romantic valley of the Black Mountains, to the right of the Abergavenny road. Founded as a priory early in the twelfth century, it quickly rose to great fame. Calamities followed, and after passing through various hands the priory was purchased by Walter Savage Landor. The buildings, except those that now serve as an inn, are all completely ruined. An unforgettable experience awaits those who pursue their way by the waters of the Afon Honddu and light, almost suddenly, on this relic of monastic splendour lying below the lonely heights. From Pontrilas Station the River Monnow can be crossed and followed until, at Monmouth, the famous but nevertheless magnificent Wye Valley stretch of road is joined. The Vale of Tintern from the hills, and the Wye from the Wyndcliff, are two of the finest sights in the world.

ROUTE 11

MELTON MOWBRAY, the capital of the world as far as hunting is concerned, stands in a grass country divided by hedges. When cub hunting begins, and November days come, the town is completely stirred by the spirit of the chase. Out

LLANTHONY ABBEY.

MID DIVISION

of the season, Melton is just a characteristic English place, to be remembered especially for its magnificent church, and a few old houses by the churchyard. To the north of Melton Mowbray are the hills, known as the Leicestershire wolds, that extend down from Belvoir to the river valleys of the Soar and the Wreake. Although not of great height, they give many pleasant scenes of wooded and open country, broken by fairly steep falls leading to the surrounding plains.

Villages and tiny hamlets, frequently known by Danish names, square church towers, and the farmhouses and cottages of an agricultural community are scattered over the slopes of this region, so inviting for leisurely wandering.

The Nottingham highway from Melton Mowbray mounts up to Broughton Hill crossroads. To the right is the undulating country towards Belvoir, and the turning to the left follows the ridge to Six Hills, a place famous for the meets of the Quorn. Here, running north and south, is the Fosse Way. In a remote village, under the hills, is the exceptionally picturesque old hall of Ragdale, one of those country homes that ever appeal to the imagination. It tells of the days of the Shirleys who lived in it, generation following generation, from the time of Queen Elizabeth. This house, shewing a succession of varied outlines and textures capped by irregular gables and clustered chimneys, presents a perfect harmony of colour and beauty when seen from the churchyard adjoining.

A few miles past Six Hills is the descent to the wide valley of the Soar. The large villages of Barrow and Quorndon, occupying opposite banks of the stream, are divided by the park of Quorndon Hall, where Hugo Meynell, that great rider and father of modern fox-hunting, made his headquarters from 1754. The big woods of Mount Sorrel loom ahead. Further on, after crossing the busy Leicester-Loughborough highway and proceeding towards Woodhouse, the bold ridges of Charnwood Forest come into view. Charnwood, from Grace Dieu to Bradgate, appears as a small enclosed country, peculiar in its geology and landscape. It is full of hills that rise up sharply to considerable heights—Bardon is over 900 feet—and their topmost shapes are rendered curious by exposed crags and isolated rocks. These lofty features give a romantic appearance to the landscape, which includes, as well, a great deal of wood and bracken. Unfortunately, most of the view-points are in private hands, but it is worth while making the climb to the windmill at Woodhouse Eaves.

At the top of the ascent under Beacon Hill, the left-hand forest way for Newtown Linford passes by the beautiful expanse of Bradgate deer park, where another extensive prospect will be seen by those who follow the pathway up to Old John Tower. At Bradgate Lady Jane Grey was born—the house has almost gone—and a second royal lady, Elizabeth Woodville, once lived close by at Groby. The old Hall is situated below the church on the far side of Groby Pool. Form here to Ratby, in reach of the Tudor Kirby Muxloe Castle, and past the brickwork of Desford Old Hall, leads to yet another scene of royal consequence, Market Bosworth.

Bosworth Field, on which King Richard III lost his crown and his life, is between the villages of Sutton Cheney and Shenton.

The route from Bosworth town, through Twycross, follows a ridge overlooking the Midland Plain. It skirts the park of Gopsal Hall, built by Charles Jennens, the Birmingham magnate and patron of Handel, passes the two Applebys, Magna and Parva—note the manor, old houses, and Sir Christopher Wren's Grammar School—and swings left, then right, by the fine church spire of Clifton Campville, into the level valley of the Tame, and that of the Trent, which is followed through Armitage and Rugeley to Stafford. By easy going the way then continues through Penkridge, along the Watling Street to a mile past Weston Park, turns right for Newport, and, after a sharp rise to the west of this town, approaches Shrewsbury by Edgmond, High Ercall, and Haughmond Hill. This stretch of England, from Market Bosworth to Shrewsbury, is real Midland country. It is flat in parts, pleasing without being spectacular, and is not devoid of hills and broken grounds. Although the coal-mining districts round Nuneaton, Brownhills, Cannock, and to the east of Wellington, have to be avoided, there is much elsewhere to be seen through the miles of pastoral landscape—Tamworth Castle and town, once the seat of Mercian Kings; the spires of Dr. Johnson's City of Lichfield; pretty villages like King's Bromley, the Ridwares (including Hamstall Ridware manor-house) and Abbot's Bromley; high-placed Hanbury in Needwood Forest; Tutbury Castle, rising over the waters of the River Dove, within whose walls, now ruined, Mary Queen of Scots spent sad days of imprisonment; Beaudesert Park, delightful for walks among the bracken; the succession of lovely estates and woods bordering the northern heathery moorlands of Cannock Chase; timbered houses in Greengate Street, Stafford, and at Penkridge; Boscobel House, near to Watling Street, where Charles II hid after the battle of Worcester; the trees and hills surrounding the notable village of Tong; and the abbey ruins of Lilleshall and Haughmond.

The end of this journey is perhaps its best part, for it leads to great attractions. Shrewsbury, already a large and ancient place when the Conqueror's kinsman Roger de Montgomery built his castle there, and near to which in later days Harry Hotspur was slain (Battlefield church lies four miles to the north), is comparable to Chester and the old parts of Coventry. Its buildings and houses of stone and timber and brickwork are so remarkable, and there is such a picturesque combination of weathered masonry and churches, timbered mansions, winding streets, and Jacobean and

CANNOCK CHASE FROM MILFORD HILL.

eighteenth-century fronts, that no nook or corner should be left unexplored all the way between Castle Gates, Town Walls, the Welsh Bridge and Abbey Foregate. Associations abound; Richmond lodged in the black-and-white house in Wyle Cop on his way to Bosworth Field; the shops in Butcher Row, together with the house of the Abbots of Lilleshall, give a picture of a fifteenth-century street; an ornate gateway off Castle Street originally led to the Council House of the Court of the Marches of Wales; the names of the splendid town mansions recall Shropshire families; Shrewsbury cakes, mediæval in origin, were made by Pailin at the shop on the corner of School Lane; the Restoration dramatist Farquhar, whom nobody reads, wrote plays at the now modernised Raven Hotel; "Thomas Ingoldsby" conceived a bloodthirsty legend of "Shrewsberrie"; from the Lion yard at the top of Wyle Cop, the celebrated Wonder coach regularly covered the 158 miles to London in fifteen hours and three-quarters; and running north-west from the Welsh Bridge is Telford's great Holyhead road.

On leaving Shrewsbury by St. Giles, and taking the course of the River Severn, Wroxeter is reached. Here are the ruins of the great Roman city of Uriconium, which occupied a site at the junction of Watling Street and the Roman highway controlling the Welsh frontier. Roman columns form the gate-piers in Wroxeter churchyard. The Wrekin, away to the left, commands from its 1,300 ft. summit an unusually extensive field of view. After the very pretty village of Leighton comes the stonework of Buildwas Abbey in a glorious setting, followed by a crossing over the bridge leading to the 400 feet ascent up to the sweet little town and abbey of Much Wenlock. With yet another rise the road almost touches a height of 800 feet. Then, gradually dropping between Wenlock Edge and Brown Clee Hill, it keeps to the stream and meadows of Corve Dale, passes the sixteenth-century gables and broad bays of Shipton Hall, just avoids De Clifford's Cortham Castle and Fair Rosamund's Well behind Diddlebury village, nears the moated house of Elsick down in the fields by the Craven Arms turning, and finally mounts up to the big church and castle of Ludlow. This district is one of superlative beauty. Ludlow, with its bold hillside situation, its inns, and its quaint steep byways, is a wonderful place. One of England's most remarkable fortified houses stands at Stokesay. The delights of Wenlock Edge are well-nigh inexhaustible, whether they be sought in the woods and commons, between banks of spring primroses, or among the sundry old buildings, such as the almost unique thirteenth-century forest house at Upper Millichope, and Wilderhope Manor just below the crest of the ridge. Away to the north-west, over Church Stretton, are the lines of Caradoc and the Long Mynd, and the peaks of Wales. Bishop's Castle is in the midst of very fine country, the upper Teme Valley is full of rugged beauty, while due west of Craven Arms, as the local rhyme tells,

"Clunton and Clunbury, Clungunford and Clun
Are the prettiest places under the sun."

This land of the Welsh Marches, through which the Romans had a line of hill forts, Offa his Dyke, and the Conqueror his chain of castles, abounds in legend and romance. It is full

LUDLOW FROM WHITCLIFF.

of suggestion in its names and configuration, as any one will find who wanders through dreamy Clun to Bicton, and climbs up the mountain to the height by Shadwell Hall. Steep valleys lie below it and mountains stretch beyond. Offa's Dyke can be seen following the contours towards Montgomery. Camps and ditches and tumuli, reminiscent of strife and tribal war, crown many of the eminences, and they stand up strangely amidst the stillness that now belongs to Clun Forest and the Black Mountain.

ROUTE 12

MOST of Cheshire is either too flat, or too busy-looking, to be really picturesque. Away from the towns and the outlying areas of Manchester, it is a country of prosperous farms and good roads. But the chief interest of the district lies in its timbered buildings, elaborately constructed in oak and plaster, that shew up in strong contrasts of black and white against a trim and orderly landscape. These old houses and cottages, with their massive angle-posts, overhanging storeys, complex woodwork, and carved beams and brackets, are instances of an architectural style that originated and developed through an abundant supply of fine oak. The forests of Cheshire, once numbered among the most extensive in England, provided the material for building which the excellent carpenters of the fifteenth and sixteenth centuries used to good purpose. Work of vigorous design was erected, with each timber serving a definite constructional end, and it was often enriched with curious and almost fantastic wood patterns. These black-and-white houses, heritages of the past, and characteristic

PLATE XIII.

THROUGH CHARNWOOD FOREST.

CHURCH STRETTON AND THE LONG MYND.

PLATE XIV.

Monsal Dale, Derbyshire.

Birkland Forest, Edwinstowe.

CHESTER 77

features in the Cheshire scene, have always appealed to the hearts of the English people. Chester, situated at the commencement of this tour, is full of them. They are to be found near and within the walls that completely surround the city—in Watergate and Bridge Streets, above the

MORETON OLD HALL AND GATEHOUSE.

low galleries of the Rows, in the old houses that belonged to county families when Chester had its "season," and along the byways that visitors from all the world over come to see. The "Bear and Billet," the "Falcon," and several other old hostelries are notable. It was at the "Yacht Inn," quite near to Bishop Lloyd's House, that Dean Swift stayed when he invited the Cathedral dignitaries to have supper with him; their refusal to do so was commemorated by the satirist in the following words, which he scratched on a window with a diamond ring:

> "Mouldy without—rotten within,
> The church and the clergy are all near akin."

Other house-fronts, not more than two hundred years old, conceal ancient panelling, oak chimney-pieces and elaborate ceilings. Below the present city are remains of religious establishments, and beneath them lie buried the ruins of an important Roman town.

GAWSWORTH HALL.

The old London coach route from Chester, passing through pretty Tarporley, leads through pleasant agricultural country to Highwayside. From this point Sandbach may be reached along the byways running to the left for Wettenhall, to the right and left for Minshull and Minshull Vernon station, and beyond the station to the right again for Occlestone Green and Stud Green. Here are good forward roads to Sandbach and Congleton. Black-and-white houses will be seen here and there among the dairy-farms and the trees, as well as in the two towns mentioned above. The most notable of them all, Moreton Old Hall, a remarkable structure dating from the first years of Queen Elizabeth's reign, is a little south of Congleton, beyond Astbury. Further north, lying within the country stretching towards Manchester, many other interesting timbered buildings are to be found—churches at Marton, Lower Peover and Warburton, houses at Gawsworth, Prestbury, Woodford, Handforth, Mobberley, in the Alderley neighbourhood, and in the little town of Knutsford, which was depicted in Mrs. Gaskell's *Cranford*. But the old houses are rapidly disappearing. Demolition proceeds apace—the fine house of Marton has now been pulled down—and all who wish to see them must act quickly, before it is too late.

At Congleton rise the hills, outliers of the Pennine Range, which occupies the whole of northern Staffordshire and Derbyshire. In direct contrast to the Cheshire Plain, they embrace rugged scenes, and offer wide distant prospects over mountains and dales. The heights are bleak and desolate; limestone cliffs and crags figure boldly in the romantic ravines. Clear streams, homes of wily trout, course rapidly between rocky banks that are often luxuriant with vegetation and woods. The villages, built entirely of stone, straggle down the hillsides, or occupy sheltered positions below the slopes. Throughout the region will be found all the elements of impressive landscape, enriched here and there with places full of historical associations. Roads, as may be expected, have hills in plenty, and all who go awheel from Congleton towards the highlands need to have sound engines and good brakes.

When the exceedingly steep climb, commencing a mile past Congleton, has been negotiated, Ryecroft Gate and Leek are reached, to be followed by a crossing over the Staffordshire highlands to Hartington. The lovely Manifold valley, and the famous Dove Dale, are close at hand. From "Newhaven Inn" comes a long drop to Youlgreave, with the picturesque village of Alport lying below. Far above are Stanton in the Peak, and the long, low front of Stanton Old Hall. The valley way ends in the Bakewell Road. Turning to the left, Haddon Hall will be seen among the greenery that borders the River Wye. Beyond Bakewell and Ashford, Monsal Dale opens out, to be explored only on foot. Further ahead, a left-hand turning, after leaving the big church of Tideswell away to the left, leads to the bleak Peak Forest district. Onward from Sparrow Pit cross-roads, the route under the Peak, rising to 1,400 feet, is continued to Peveril's ruined castle, crowning a steep spur under which the town of Castleton lies. Here the river valley is followed to Hathersage, Grindleford Bridge and Baslow, where the way to Chatsworth lies straight ahead. Two interesting villages, Eyam and Stoney Middleton, are worth seeing by a short detour to the right. A left-hand turning from Baslow—after providing a climb to the top of East Moor—gives views towards Chesterfield's twisted leaden spire.

To reach the Dukeries means crossing a short stretch of

REYNARD'S CAVE, DOVEDALE.

coalfield at Chesterfield and proceeding to Bolsover. This small town, noted for a castle that was the scene of much magnificence, is not far distant from the massive Elizabethan mansion of

"Hardwick Hall
More glass than wall."

At Cuckney, The Dukeries stretch eastwards. They are bounded by the roads connecting Worksop, Osberton, and Ollerton. The great houses they include are well known— Welbeck Abbey, Worksop Manor, Osberton Hall, Clumber

House, Thoresby Hall and Rufford Abbey. Within the parks and woodlands, and particularly in the neighbourhood of Birkland Forest, between Edwinstowe and Budby, ancient trees, magnificent avenues, and shady winding paths through scenes of wild natural beauty, suggest the grandeur that once belonged to the Sherwood Forest of Robin Hood.

DIVISION IV

EASTERN ENGLAND

(Shewn on Map Facing Introduction, p. viii)

The area of this eastern section is determined by a line taken from Ipswich, through Cambridge, to a point below St. Neots on the Great North Road; by the Great North Road itself; and by the Humber and the eastern coast-line. The chief main routes are from Cambridge to Lincoln and the Humber, through Peterborough, with a branch to Spalding, Boston, Louth, and Grimsby; to King's Lynn through Ely; to Norwich by Newmarket and Thetford, with a branch to Bury St. Edmund's and Ipswich; to Norwich from Ipswich, with branches to Cromer and Wells; and the coast road from Lowestoft and Yarmouth, to Cromer, Wells, and King's Lynn, which continues round the Wash to Long Sutton, Boston, Wainfleet, and Skegness. There are also excellent cross-roads, such as those from Gainsborough to Louth, Grantham to Spilsby, Peterborough to Wisbech and King's Lynn, and quite a network of them in Norfolk and Suffolk. The surfaces of such roads are usually good. Runs of level miles are encountered throughout the Fens and round the Broads. There is a certain hilliness north and south of Lincoln, and in the Wolds. Slopes, not very steep, occur through Norfolk and Suffolk, and east and west of Cambridge. The side roads in Norfolk and Suffolk are liable to become rough with sharp loose flints. In the marsh country there are byways and tracks, divided by gates, running by the sides of dykes. Numerous tracks and green ways are met with in the hilly parts of Lincolnshire.

The geology of the area includes the wide chalk belt in Norfolk and Suffolk, chalk to the east of the Lincolnshire

INTRODUCTION

Wolds, the oolitic limestone extending from the Humber to the Ouse, and clays and sands in the neighbourhoods of the Wash and the Norfolk and Suffolk coast. The landscape in the district of the Fens is dominated by high and often windy skies. Although flat, it has all the charm that comes from wide open expanses, miles of productive land, long belts of trees, and straight dykes and waterways. Similar conditions prevail in the country of the Broads. The higher lands of Norfolk and Suffolk are richly wooded, and show an unending panorama of pastoral scenery. In the undulating parts of Lincolnshire there are green-clad slopes and grassy uplands, from which may be seen long stretches of far-distant country. By the sea, and away from such populated parts as Lowestoft, Yarmouth, and Cromer, much of the coastline is full of beauty. Cultivated fields extend right down to the salty marshes and golden sands of the coast. All round the Wash, and along the northern sea-board of Norfolk, are solitary places thronged with wild birds, where visitors, other than the local gatherers of shell-fish, rarely penetrate.

Evidences of early history survive in the track known as Peddars Way, that can be traced through lonely country south of Hunstanton. Icknield Street, running north-east from Newmarket, and such villages as Icklingham, near Mildenhall, preserve the name of the Tribe of Iceni, who held Norfolk and Suffolk prior to the Roman Conquest. Roman days are recalled by the Ermine and Fosse Ways, the Norwich Way, and the Cambridgeshire Via Devana; by the sea-banks, near Wisbech, erected to keep back the waters of the Wash; by the masonry at Lincoln, Horncastle and Burgh Castle, Yarmouth, and by many other tracks and remains. After the Dark Ages, and in spite of frequent ravages by the Danes, the whole district from Lincoln to Norwich became a seat of ecclesiasticism, by reason of which there gradually arose the wonderful chain of cathedrals and abbeys that is still one of the glories of this land. To the activities of the monks, also, was due the early system of draining and cultivating the fens and marshes. There are great castles at Newark, Lincoln, Castle Rising, Framlingham and elsewhere, and a number of fine mediæval bridges. Hereward the Wake, in his stand against William the Conqueror in the neighbourhood of Ely, furnished an historic interlude. King John, too, is another figure of these eastern roads; travelling with his army at a speed that seems almost incredible for the year 1216—in one week alone he covered 225 miles—he marched rapidly up and down Lincolnshire, only to be overtaken by disaster at the Wash. The settlement of weavers from the Low Countries, the rise and decline of the cloth industry in Norfolk and Suffolk, trading intercourse with the Continent, and the activities of Dutch drainage engineers, are other events that have left their mark in various ways on this part of the country.

Architecturally, the district is remarkably rich in ecclesiastical buildings. There are the cathedrals of Lincoln, Peterborough, Ely, and Norwich, many abbeys, fine churches such as Lavenham, Boston and Louth, the Lincolnshire village spires, and the decorated stone-and-flint towers and porches of Norfolk and Suffolk. To the west of Lincolnshire, the stone bed provided the building material for the old towns and villages, but here the rural work is neither so good nor as interesting as will be found elsewhere. Nearer the coast, and all the way across Cambridgeshire, Norfolk and Suffolk, plaster, brick and timber, and a certain amount of flint are the local materials of the domestic dwellings. Thatching of outstanding merit is frequently seen. The woodwork is often rich and finely executed; plaster walls shew surface patterning and modelled reliefs, and a very interesting phase of flint building can be studied in the houses and cottages of the north Norfolk coast. Some of the early examples of English brickwork survive in the old halls and manor-houses, among which Tattershall Castle, East Barsham Hall, and Gedding Hall may be mentioned as notable. Foreign immigrants and trading relations with the Low Countries influenced the development of style in brickwork, so there is often a suggestion of Holland or Flanders in the picturesque groups of gables. They are particularly evident throughout the Fens, in the eastern districts of Norfolk and Suffolk and in such towns as Boston, Spalding, King's Lynn, and Yarmouth. But almost every country town, whether it now be flourishing or decayed, has its own beautiful buildings that recall former prosperous days.

SUFFOLK

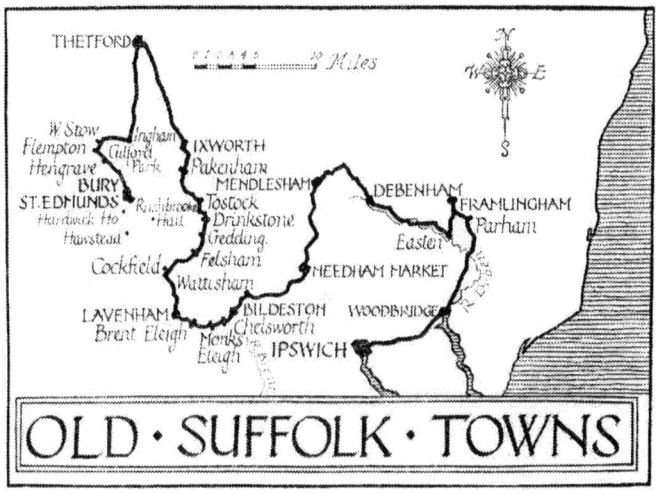

ROUTE 13

THE Woolsack in the House of Lords was not, of course, placed there by accident. It appears to have had its origin in Elizabethan times, when the exportation of wool in the raw state was forbidden. Its purpose was to remind the Lord Chancellor of the source of England's wealth and prosperity. There is quite a connection between the Woolsack and the East Anglian towns, for the fortunes of Norfolk and Suffolk were for centuries intimately connected with the manufacture of wool. In quite early days Flemish artisans were encouraged to settle in England to develop the woollen industry. As long ago as the thirteenth century they were at Worstead in Norfolk, and after that time many skilful immigrants came from the Low Countries to live and work in our Eastern Counties. A great cloth trade thus came into being. Norwich was its centre, and from the fourteenth century to the seventeenth, Norfolk and Suffolk were among the chief manufacturing counties of England. The consequent influx of wealth affected the whole district, while the presence of foreign settlers, and trading intercourse with the Low Countries, brought new influences to local life. These conditions were reflected in the ecclesiastical and domestic architecture. Many great churches—such as those of Lavenham and St. Lawrence, Ipswich—owed their existence to the munificence of the wool-traders. They were enriched with craftwork, in stone and wood, that was executed as finely as that on the Continent. In houses the Dutch or Flemish manner of building in brick was followed, at a time when the use of bricks was not common elsewhere in England.

A DOORWAY IN THETFORD.

Evidences of the times and conditions that now have gone may still be seen throughout Suffolk, in towns and churches, in houses with corbie-stepped and curved gables, and in the peculiar bonding of much old brickwork.

Bury St. Edmund's, standing at the junction of a number of high-roads, makes a good starting-point. It shews many interesting things; remains of one of the most magnificent of English abbeys, Moyse's Hall of the twelfth century, old houses and open spaces, and the "Angel" coaching inn, where Mr. Pickwick became the victim of the artful Jingle. Within a few miles will be found excellent examples of domestic architecture—Hardwick House, of 1681, the moated Elizabethan Rushbrooke Hall, and the drawbridge at Hawstead. The Mildenhall road from Bury goes by Hengrave Hall and church. The house was built early in the sixteenth century, and above the entrance is a triple oriel window, with much enrichment. Seen from the church-yard, many stone turrets and battlemented walls make a really impressive picture. The church contains a series of remarkably good carved and coloured tombs with recumbent figures under canopies. Beyond Hengrave, the right-hand turning at Flempton church passes by pine trees and

Culford Park to West Stow. Here, just beyond the church, away to the left, appears the singular brick gateway of West Stow Hall. At Ingham, the next village, the main Bury road makes a straight line for the open heaths and pine trees of Thetford.

Thetford, just over the Norfolk border, and once known for its wool fair, should be seen. From there to Ixworth, and on to Lavenham and Needham Market through the lanes, is rural Suffolk at its best, where many oak trees, luxuriant wildflowers, and white thatched cottages figure prominently.

GEDDING HALL.

Pakenham has all the charm of a real English village, and after the main Stowmarket road has been crossed at Tostock (here following the signpost for Drinkstone), the narrow lanes are always quiet and peaceful. Two miles from Drinkstone, after winding between hedgerows, the old Hall of Gedding appears. It stands away beyond a grassy space, below which a little stream flows. Mellow brickwork turning grey with age, a moat, narrow casements, and irregular time-worn limes, give to this ancient pile an air of romance and mystery. The standing walls are but a relic of what once was there. Only the gatehouse has survived the ravages of the centuries, but its patterned brickwork is very beautiful. And after Gedding, Lavenham, to be reached by Felsham and Cockfield. In many ways Lavenham still retains the characteristics and semblance of a Tudor town. It has whole streets of timber-framed houses, with carved angle-posts, barge-boards, and decorative plaster reliefs, two remarkable timbered halls, and a great church on a hill, all bearing witness to the prosperous days of the woollen trade.

A YARD IN DEBENHAM, SUFFOLK.

Down Water Street, the picturesque valley road to Bildeston embraces a chain of exceptionally attractive villages, where a succession of cottages and farms, sometimes lining the highway and sometimes standing amidst willows and alders, continually delights the eye. The place-names are Brent Eleigh, Monks Eleigh, Chelsworth, and finally Bildeston, which last is a small old town. Observe its overhanging gables, its oaken houses, and the Crown Hotel on a cobbled bank. Within this inn may be seen moulded beams of great length and girth, as well as much timber-work. The right-hand turning, for Wattisham, ascends the hill and continues over level country until the long street of Needham Market is reached.

Beyond the Bull Inn, with a carved Gothic angle-post, and at the first right-hand turning past Needham Church (note its lofty hammer-beam roof) signposts direct first to Mendlesham, and then to Debenham, two old decayed Suffolk towns. Both are now secluded, and seem to be far away from the modern world. But they were not always so. Mendlesham's church, elaborate with patterning in

PLATE XV.

LAVENHAM.

BRENT ELEIGH.

MENDLESHAM

PLATE XVI.

KIRSTEAD OLD HALL.

LITTLE WALSINGHAM GREEN.

ACROSS HICKLING BROAD.

stone and split-flint, and its two remaining streets testify to days of prosperity long since gone. Debenham, too, was once a market town, and its guildhall still stands among groups of picturesque houses that bulge and overhang into the roadways. Framlingham, another similar place, is most pleasantly reached by Deben's stream, which is forsaken at the turning by Easten Park. It had a huge castle, now ruined, that was the scene of brave days when Princess Mary, in 1553, proclaimed herself Queen. But a few miles away is Parham Old Hall, rising upward from a broad moat. It has timbering and more brickwork of an early date, built by Sir Christopher de Parham between 1498 and 1527. The old Yarmouth coach-road is next gained, and beyond Woodbridge—a fascinating little town—is the port of Ipswich, with Wolsey's brick gateway, Sparrow's House of elaborate plasterwork in the Butter Market, and other ancient bits tucked away among things modern.

ROUTE 14

NORWICH, no doubt has altered a good deal since George Borrow knew it, or "Old Crome" painted on Mousehold Heath, but apart from the obvious sights—" its thrice twelve churches . . . a grey old castle on the top of that mighty mound . . . that old Norman master-work, that cloud-encircled cathedral spire"—many bits of the old city remain. They are hidden away in odd corners and need to be looked for. In the narrow streets and alleys that lie near the precincts of the Cathedral, or round the Market Place, many a gable and archway and house-front tell of history from Tudor to Georgian times. On market days, too, the animated present lives in the throng of Norfolk country-folk that crowd the square. A mile away, at Heigham, is the Dolphin Inn, reached by the Dereham and Old Palace roads. It is a splendid specimen of flint and stone building, is dated 1587, 1595, and 1615, and was formerly the home of Bishop Hall, the satirist and divine, who suffered imprisonment under the Long Parliament.

All round Norwich is a country of fields and farms. It is well wooded, and the roads and lanes lead to unspoiled villages where old customs and associations linger. Among the village people hereabout are remarkable characters, and often will be seen the Norfolk farmer, sturdy and tanned, clothed in brown coat, breeches and light gaiters. In secluded places are many old houses with excellent brickwork, and fine thatching continually shows on the roofs of cottages and great barns.

The heart of the country is quickly reached from Norwich Post Office by the Beccles road. At the top of Trowse hill the right turning for Bungay goes by Arminghall—where, alas, Master William Ely's house, of 1487, has recently been destroyed—and after passing Poringland, and entering Brooke, a left-hand lane goes to Kirstead Old Hall, with crew-stepped gables and walls of diapered brickwork. It is now a farm, but wonderfully well preserved. By returning to the Bungay road, and crossing it, signposts can be followed through rural lanes to the Saxlinghams, past Newton Flotman, to Florden's Elizabethan Hall. Onward again, with the landscape on all sides pastoral and rich, to the main Norwich road, and from there, by a left-hand turning, to the timbered market cross and the noble twin towers of Wymondham.

A pretty way goes from Wymondham, by Kimberley Park, to Barnham Broom, where may be seen another old Norfolk brick house, with a crow-stepped porch, and a heavily panelled oaken door under an arched opening. Northwards, beyond the weather-boarded mills of the River Yare, is a good road for East Dereham, an ancient though thriving place. Here the poet Cowper died; here, also, was the scene of George Borrow's birth and the opening chapter of *Lavengro*—" On an evening of July, in the year 18—, at East D——, a beautiful little town in a certain district of East Anglia, I first saw the light." After East Dereham the route continues to Guist, bears to the left beyond the River Wensum, reaches Fakenham, where the right-hand road goes through arable and wooded country, rich with wild flowers in summer, to East Barsham. As a hill is descended the towers and turrets and clustered chimneys of the Hall appear between the trees. At the foot of the hill a most memorable picture is revealed in the highly ornamented brickwork enriched with terra-cotta ornaments, archways and mouldings that cast deep shadows, many embattlements, and moulded turrets and chimneys, all coloured by weather and age. The house belongs to the time of Henry VII, and is one of the most remarkable instances of the early use of bricks in England. A signpost by the neighbouring brook directs to the narrow lane for Great Snoring. Behind the church is the rectory, once the manor-house of Sir Ralph Shelton. It was built about the year 1500, and its existing walls and towers, with tracery in the late Perpendicular style, are hardly less interesting than those of East Barsham.

Down the vale to Little Walsingham is pretty all the way. The little town, now but a fraction of its former size, has a great past. When it was celebrated throughout Christendom as a place of pilgrimage, kings and queens and princes came to pay homage at the Shrine of Our Lady of Walsingham. The last English monarch to tread the way barefoot from the slipper chapel at North Barsham to the shrine was Henry VIII. But bluff King Hal, his penitential devotions being over, soon caused the image to be removed and publicly burned in London. Thus came to an end the prosperous days of Walsingham and its Priory. Beyond the Priory gate and ruins, an old well and beacon, and timbered houses, lies the road to Wells. Four miles to the east are the impressive ruins of Binham Abbey. Passing cultivated lands and cornfields, that extend almost down to the waters of the sea, the coastline is gained. Here are famous haunts of wild birds, notably the terns, and at certain seasons of the year many birds, flying high, almost blacken the sky, and fill the air with their plaintive notes.

THE RECTORY, GREAT SNORING.

The good coast road eastwards from Wells is always attractive. First it reaches the village of Stiffkey, a little gem of a place, with wooded uplands, a winding stream, and, in the long days, a profusion of willow herb, mallow, wild convolvulus, purple vetch and flowering nettle. There is also a picturesque hall by the church, once the home of Sir Nicholas Bacon, Queen Elizabeth's Lord Keeper, and father of the noble Francis; natives, in confidential vein, still relate that Shakespeare's plays first saw light within these walls! The houses and cottages here, as well as throughout this district, are quite remarkable for their flintwork, laid in straight courses, or shaped into patterns and curly gables.

Further on from Stiffkey come views over the sea, marshes intersected with winding channels, and the long sinuous stretch of land ending in Blakeney Point. High on a hill is Blakeney church with a chancel beacon, a conspicuous landmark for miles around. By sea and marsh, cultivated hills rising inland, and more grey flint walls at Cley and Salthouse, the route mounts the hill to Weybourne, where the character of the landscape changes when the turning by the church, for

CLEY AND BLAKENEY CHURCH.

Holt, is taken. The hills become steeper, and they are crowned with pine trees. Ling and bracken grow in profusion, and the open commons are glorious with purple bloom in August.

The Norwich highway follows Holt's main street, then winds by heaths and undulating country to Saxthorpe—and beware the rough surface of the road. Here is a left turning for Aylsham, the Bure to be crossed, and soon the shady wooded glades of Blickling's Park are gained. Blickling is truly one of the stately homes of England. It is steeped in historical associations; once the seat of the Boleyn family, it was here that the ill-fated Ann spent her childhood. The present building dates from the time of James I. Standing away from the road beyond green lawns, banks of old yew, and high trees, its fanciful outlines ever delight the eye. Aylsham, two miles away and on the River Bure, is a gateway to the land of the Norfolk Broads, where level roads and lanes lead by winding rivers and open waters, bordered by reeds. This scenery of wide expanses and open skies has a peculiar charm of its own, and the landscape is always enlivened by the bright sails of small craft travelling in the breeze.

POTTER HEIGHAM BRIDGE.

Beyond Aylsham Station the road is never far away from the river all the way to Wroxham. On its route a number of old houses may be discovered, notably Oxnead's Tudor Hall, and one at Little Hautbois, of Elizabethan date. The reed thatching, too, shews conspicuously on many a cottage and barn. The signpost for Yarmouth, at Wroxham, directs really into the heart of the Broads, which lie in the neighbourhood of Hoveton and Horning. Not far from this last-named place is St. Benet's Abbey gateway, a ruin belonging to an establishment that tradition dates back to the days of King Canute. The Yarmouth road continues past Ludham to Potter Heigham, where once was a Roman pottery. The church of this village shews, in its round tower, thatched roof, timber ceiling, and painted wooden rood screen, characteristic features that may be looked for elsewhere in East Anglia. By the side of the churchyard is a path, through sedges and marsh, and a veritable haunt of dragon-flies, to the secluded waters of Hickling Broad. A short distance from Potter Heigham is the old bridge over the Thurne, a right-hand turn for Acle, more marshes dotted with windmills, and then Acle itself, approached through an avenue of willows. Two miles along the Norwich road from Acle is a signpost directing to Lingwood Station. By following it and taking the second turning on the left, the manor-house of South Burlingham may be reached. It is now a farm with a long thatched roof; and its former importance is evident by the fine brick porch, flanked by octagonal turrets. And so, from here, back to Norwich by pretty Blofield, or eastward through the marsh to Yarmouth's old houses and " Rows," and haunts of " David Copperfield," and on by the coast to Walberswick and decayed Dunwich.

ROUTE 15

CAMBRIDGE is a good starting point for the discovery of the Fens. Of the town itself no enthusiastic traveller can ever tire, nor cease to find delight in its courts and gateways that link past with present. But all who go there will gather their own impressions as they wander by College lawns and gardens, and cross the bridges that connect the leafy banks of the River Cam. Not far from Bridge Street and Magdalene College is the turning for Ely. After passing Milton, the way over the fen, once Roman, rises to Stretham's ancient cross, where the first glimpse of Ely's towers and incomparable lantern is obtained. The Island of Ely, which was the scene of Hereward the Wake's memorable stand against the Conqueror, is entirely surrounded by low fen. Even now, the conquest of the waters in the neighbourhood of the Little Ouse is an ever-present difficulty and danger. Fen life under such conditions is therefore trying, and the people of the locality, who are great workers, have peculiar characteristics that, doubtless, have been largely determined by the hardships imposed by natural forces.

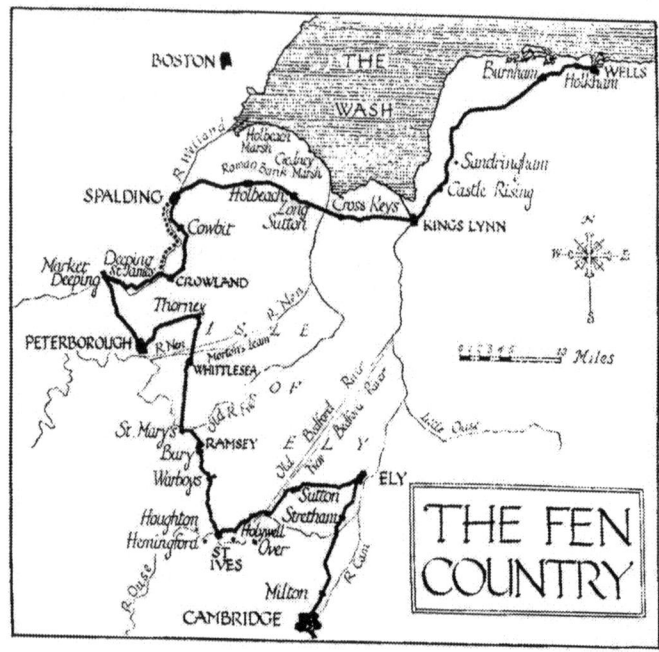

Cromwell's house at Ely must look much as it did when he lived there, and on the green in front of it the future Protector commenced to train the men who were to become his Ironsides. Ely to Sutton, and by the two unique Bedford Rivers —cut in 1630 and 1650 to drain the Fens—leads to the valley of the Ouse and St. Ives. For all who love lush meadows, water-mills, and slow winding streams, this tract has everything to offer between the villages of Over, Holywell, Hemingford, and Houghton. The way into St. Ives, after two sharp turns, enters the town at the open market. Here it bears to the right and proceeds along the perfectly flat Market Hill, past Theodore Watts-Dunton's house, the "Lion" yard with creeper-clad balconies, and Oliver Cromwell's monument (he was a townsman from 1631-36). On no account fail to make a slight detour at the Cambridge

THE FENS

turning to see the mediæval bridge spanning the Ouse—an impressive picture of pointed arches and stone cut-waters, mirrored in liquid reflections. Signposts point to the up-and-down road for Ramsey, via Warboys and Bury's high church tower. Opposite Ramsey church are fragments of the Abbey, rich in Perpendicular carving and panelling.

Ramsey's wide Great Whyte, proceeding north-west, leads to the old River Nen until, at St. Mary's, the right turning goes straight to Whittlesea and Thorney. This is one of the roads over the Bedford Level, one of the great examples of skill in the reclamation of marshland. As long ago as the days of the Romans, and later, in the times of the monks, isolated parts of the marsh were drained. Bishop Morton, about 1480, began work on a larger scale—his " Leam " will be seen from the road by Whittlesea—but the subsequent suppression of the Abbeys brought to an end the good efforts of the churchmen, and the waters once more gained control. It was not until the seventeenth century that a comprehensive scheme for draining the Fens was formed; it was planned and put into operation by the Dutchman, Cornelius Vermuyden, and to him and later engineers the conquest of the Fens has been due. This marshland is a scene of wide expanses, where alders and ash trees bend to the prevailing winds. There is little shade from the sun. Coarse fish and wildfowl abound. The byways, carried on the dyke-banks, are lined with sedges and grasses and flowering plants. Isolated gates mark the passages over dykes and " drains." Here and there is a windmill, and on every hand is to be seen the rich productive soil. Although the landscape is interesting rather than particularly beautiful, it attracts by its long low lines that shew below high skies. It is strongly reminiscent of Holland, too, and Dutch architectural features shew in the peculiar gables of many brick buildings.

Whittlesea, though it has two good stone houses, a noble church spire, a picturesque butter cross, and memories of great skating days, does not altogether attract. So proceed onward between the willows, past Stone Bridge Corner, to the fine avenues over which rise Thorney's Abbey towers. When the village is reached it gives one of those little vignettes that live long in memory—a grassy space, comfortable houses, a high park wall with a hall behind, and, above thick greenery, the mellow Norman masonry that the monks raised centuries ago. Once mitred abbots cultivated their vines and orchards here, and Thorney is still, as William of Malmesbury described it in 1135, " a little paradise." At the crossing is the main road to Peterborough, a busy city, but owning one of the greatest masterpieces of Early English Art in the Cathedral's western front.

A splendid road leads ahead to Market Deeping and Deeping St. James. These two places are contiguous and they make a winding line of picturesque houses and cottages for

A BYWAY ON DEEPING FEN.

almost three miles. There is an irregular succession of gables and dormers and Georgian fronts, all of stone—for near by the oolitic formation occurs—and through Deeping St. James the River Welland flows, to be crossed half way by an old stone bridge. At the far end of the last-named village, a signpost directs, left, to the station and Crowland. So over the fen again until the lane mounts the high riverbank, which here rises above the surrounding country, and then . . . a superb view of Crowland and its Abbey lying low in the marsh. Coming to Crowland by this riverside way is to see it at its best, spread out in a green hollow, and dominated by the Abbey ruins. Its history must be read elsewhere, and the three-way bridge tells its own story of waters now gone.

Beyond Crowland is fen country *par excellence*. All who

THE WASH

do not mind a rough road should travel to Spalding by the Welland bank; for others there is the road through Cowbit. By either route, all the best characteristics of the fens are ever at hand—level miles of cultivated crops that in July and August present patchwork panoramas of variegated colours, and innumerable clumps of dark-green trees.

Spalding is entered by a tree-lined waterway, with many charming Georgian houses standing back on either side; if

THE CUSTOM HOUSE, KING'S LYNN.

it chances to be the hour, the carillon in the Market Place will ring out a quaint melody. The church, lying in a quiet spot behind the thatched "Old White Horse" inn at the Holbeach turning, has much of beauty both within and without. From the signpost on the bridge continue to Holbeach, and on to Long Sutton, which has the oldest and most perfect lead spire in England. Away to the north is the embankment thrown up by the Romans to stem the floods; bordering the Wash are Holbeach and Gedney Marshes, once sea, and now places of solitude. Between Long Sutton and Cross Keys, on the King's Lynn road, is historic ground. As far as the eye can reach are productive meadows that, years ago were nothing more than the sandy wastes of the Well stream, entirely covered by water at high tide. When the tide receded the sands might be crossed, but only by vigilance and care could the passage be made. On a day in October in 1216 a mile-long baggage train, laden with King John's treasures, attempted the way over the sands from Cross Keys, taking almost the identical line of the present road. All, as everyone knows, ended in disaster; men, wagons, horses, and treasure were overtaken by the incoming tide, and the catastrophe dealt a blow to King John from which he never recovered. Two days later he died at Newark.

The next point of interest is King's Lynn. In the vicinity of the fifteenth-century Guild Hall, with walls of chequered stone and flintwork, and near the Custom House that is quite a little masterpiece of Renaissance architecture, lived the wealthy merchant princes of other days. Their dwellings remain, and lie among winding ways and lanes and courtyards behind which were warehouses and granaries opening on to the quays. There are many peeps through archways, such as De Hooch would have loved to paint, and at every turn are reminders of olden trade and far-flung enterprise. Four miles from King's Lynn is the famous castle of Castle Rising, and a Bede House too; beyond is Royal Sandringham and a good road to the Burnhams, "Coke of Norfolk's" Holkham Park, and Wells, with the waters of the Wash never far away.

ROUTE 16

LINCOLN may be reached from several points, but the approach from Grantham quickly leads to the hilly grounds that are one of the features of the county. Although neither dramatic nor intensely spectacular, these gentle grassy slopes, crowned with many woods and churches, are truly England, and they guard valleys that in summer-time are rich with standing corn. Forsaking the Great North Road and the quaint old streets of Grantham, the way soon passes under the wooded heights of Belton Park, past the fine spire of Caythorpe church, through the long village of Welbourn, and so by Coleby, lying amidst many trees, to Lincoln.

PLATE XVII

THE BRIDGE, ST. IVES.

MARKET DEEPING.

THE HOLBEACH ROAD, SPALDING.

PLATE XVIII.

KIRTON, NEAR BRIGG.

THE WATERWAY, HORNCASTLE.

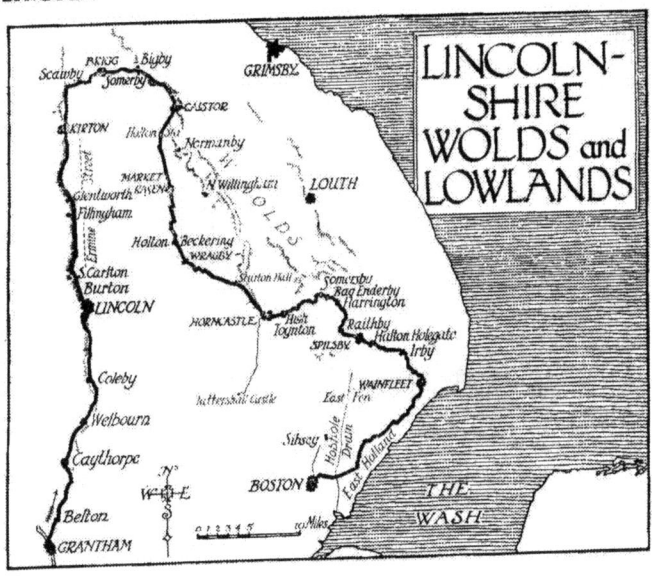

And though the hills rise on the eastern side of this road, its western boundaries are open and give quite remarkable distant views stretching far away for miles over the flat valley of the Trent. Lincoln itself is a city to see and linger in. It is very old, and most historic, while every turn reveals streets and buildings that recall days of long ago. The quiet water-way running under the bridge, with houses thereon, near the Stone Bow, the gabled dwellings, inns with sober fronts or overhanging storeys, the cobbled Steep Hill and its twelfth-century Jews' Houses, the gateways, the Conqueror's Castle, the Roman arch, and many alleys and winding footways, are all things to be remembered. And over all, dominating the city, the mighty Cathedral of the Blessed Virgin Mary rises; around it is a green close, bordered by wonderfully quaint old buildings of many dates and periods, that nestle under the shadow of the glorious fane. Here, at least, is the semblance of peace in the midst of a workaday world.

The Roman Ermine Street, with a capital modern surface, leads straight as an arrow northwards towards Brigg, but a more interesting route to this little town clings to the top of the hills west of the Roman road. Leaving the Stone Bow gate, by the Retford Road, and turning to the right at the Kirton signpost, the hilly Yarborough Road ascends the ridge and leads along the heights, past the fine park of Burton, and so to Kirton. All the way from Lincoln to Kirton there is ever a wide panorama extending away to the west and near by, at the foot of the hills, nestle many villages, each with its church and cluster of houses standing amidst cornfields and trees. Although none of them lie on the through road,

THE VALLEY AT AISTHORPE, LINCS.

almost all are worth a visit—South Carlton standing in a hollow, Fillingham with an embattled though not very old castle, Glentworth embowered in trees, and finally Kirton, a pleasant little town of narrow streets winding down to the massive Early English church tower, and possessing a windmill whose sails turn merrily on breezy days.

The ridge may be continued to the Scawby cross-roads, where a right-hand turn leads to Brigg. Thence a level run continues until the wooded heights again appear at Bigby and Somerby. Bending southwards, and through the fine broken country of the Wolds, the road reaches the old church and pretty little town of Caistor, passes Holton Station, and traverses the green vale until the bright red pantile roofs of Market Rasen come into view. The Wolds, which hereabouts always break the eastern skyline, offer endless possibilities for exploration; almost every byway up the hills

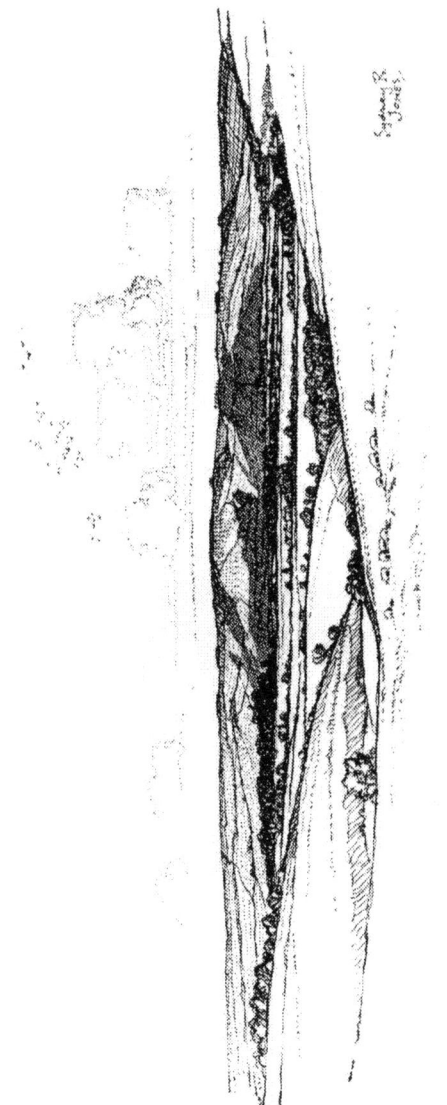

THE WOLDS BEYOND SOMERSBY.

between Normanby and North Willingham will yield its treasures. Wragby, approached by Holton Beckering, has memories of the coaching days, and just beyond its old inn the route to the right makes for Horncastle, after rising under the shade of Sturton's oaks and beech trees, where Lincoln's towers can be observed far away in the distance. Horncastle, which was once a Roman station and a castle of the Saxons, still shows traces of Roman masonry in the neigh-

BOSTON, LINCOLNSHIRE.

bourhood of the church, but the celebrated horse-fair, which used to collect as many interesting types of humanity as horses, is no longer worth an August pilgrimage. For those interested in architecture, Tattershall Castle, that splendid specimen of mid-fifteenth-century brickwork, lies some miles away to the south. A long steady climb from Horncastle ends at High Toynton Church, opposite which a left turning leads to Somersby, where in 1809, at the rectory, Alfred Tennyson was born. Beyond, through pretty winding lanes and undulating country, is Bag Enderby, Harrington's seventeenth-century hall, and southwards Raithby and

PLATE II.

COLTISHALL BROAD.

ULLSWATER FROM PLACE FELL.

LINCOLNSHIRE LOWLANDS

Spilsby, which latter place directories might designate a "neat little town." It has its glories, however, in the magnificent Willoughby monuments that lie in the church, hard by a decorated screen inscribed with melancholy words.

By good going for all things on wheels, Halton Holegate is quickly reached. Here the scene changes. The hills have gone, Boston "Stump" shews over the distant levels, and bright green meadows, and dykes, and many willow trees, combine to make the quiet beauty of the fens and marshes. Onward through Irby, the ancient port of Wainfleet, and right round by the Wash to Boston, the traveller feels as if in a foreign land. East Holland it is called, and Holland it seems to be, even though the natives are clad in English fashion. Boston itself is so fascinating, it might be Delft or Nijmegen, though its famous St. Botolph's tower cannot be matched elsewhere. Round about, too, is much of peculiar charm; flat miles of corn that shew as a sea of gold in late summer, isolated farms, thick belts of trees, the road by the Hobhole Drain, and the waterway up to Sibsey. The tale of the fens, and the dykes, and man's centuries of war with the elements, is a chapter of history well worth knowing

DIVISION V

NORTHERN ENGLAND

(Shewn on Map, facing Introduction, p. viii)

THIS section of England is enclosed by a line taken from Preston to the Humber, and by the boundary of Scotland. It is marred in parts by signs of industrial activity, and the attractions for the tourist are to be found in the dales, lakes and river valleys, and in the mountains and moors that lie away from the dull mining and manufacturing centres of Lancashire, Yorkshire, Durham and Northumberland. The area is crossed from south to north by highways, notably those serving Scotland from Carlisle and Berwick. A series of main roads give communications from east to west, examples of which are the connections between York and the Wharfe Valley, Darlington and the Lakes, and General Wade's road from Newcastle to Carlisle. Except where roads keep to the plains and river valleys, hills are frequent; in the mountainous districts of the Pennines and the Lakes they may be termed continuous, ascents and descents alternating for miles together. There are notable hill-climbs for motorists—Sutton Bank near Thirsk, and Honister Pass by Buttermere, being among the number—and the moorland and mountain section in the London-Edinburgh Run of 1926 extended from Ilkley to Tan Hill, north of Swaledale. Although many of the main mountain routes are well engineered, the gradients and surfaces of byways and tracks are often difficult to negotiate. In such places walkers have the advantage; for them there are also untrodden ways through wonderful moorland and mountain scenery.

A district characterised by highlands, it includes varied geology. The oolitic limestones of the north-east Yorkshire moors, and the chalk hills of the Wolds, rise to the east of the Plain of York. From the neighbourhood of Bradford to the Border is the carboniferous system, yielding the limestones and grits that make the rocky elevations of the Pennine Chain. Branching to the west are the silurian beds and volcanic rocks of the Lake District, giving heights such as Skiddaw and Helvellyn between the lower formations of northern Cumberland and eastern Lancashire. Where England and Scotland meet, the geological system culminates in The Cheviot. Mountains and moors, reaching to high altitudes, and the dales, lakes and rivers lying below them, give long stretches of impressive, natural scenery diversified by rocks and waterfalls, mountain passes and torrents, panoramic views, and moors covered with heather. Landscapes of this nature occur throughout the Lake District, in the Westmorland and Yorkshire Pennines, and towards the north-east coast of Yorkshire, but where Cumberland, Durham and Westmorland join, and in north-west Northumberland, the moorlands and desolate wastes become monotonous and uninteresting. The river scenes, however, are some of the most romantic in England. They include those of the Lune, Ribble, Wharfe, Ure, Nidd, Derwent and Eden, and after the rivers leave the mountains to flow through broad, fertile valleys, their banks are luxuriant with woodlands down to the water's edge. The seaboard includes the quaint fishing villages of the east coast, the beautiful bays of Runswick, Robin Hood, Filey, Bridlington and Morecambe, and Solway Firth, an inlet of wide vistas.

The story of northern England's past, largely one of feuds and wars, lives in many monuments. Hadrian's Wall, which has defied eighteen centuries of stress and storm, extends for miles through lonely, hilly country west of the North Tyne River. It tells not only of the power of the Roman Empire, but also of Caledonian tribes whose spirit was never broken. The wall was served by principal military roads and auxiliary ways, and some of their lines, as the one south of Carlisle, and the route from the Tees to Boroughbridge, have never been lost. Other links in the chain of warlike history are shewn by the walls of York, by the fortified houses, rectories, and peel-towers of Northumberland and Cumberland, and by a multitude of castles extending from Lancaster to Scarborough and on, by Durham, Alnwick, and Bamburgh, to Thirlwall and Carlisle. More suggestive of peace are the minsters of York and Beverley, and the cathedrals of Ripon and Durham, due to powerful church dignitaries who, nevertheless, were acquainted with war as well as religion. Remains of monastic establishments are numerous; those in Yorkshire—Rievaulx, Bolton, Fountains and others—are especially beautiful, both in their architecture and situations. Mediævalism and events of political significance have left their marks in such cities as York and Durham; no one visiting this last-named place can fail to be impressed by its natural position, bridges, steep streets, and the towering rock crowned with masonry, all of which have played their part in the history of bygone times. In the country the old houses are built chiefly of stone, but their style is harsher than that seen in the southern counties. The colour of the stone is cold, there are many mullions to the windows, gables are low in pitch, and roofs are covered with heavy stone slates. These old houses, however, as well as the cottages of the grey townlets and villages, have a look, a character, that admirably blends with the natural surroundings in which they are placed.

ROUTE 17

BETWEEN the Plain of York and the coastline of the North Riding is an open country of moors that extends eastwards, by a succession of elevated lands and dales, from the Hambleton and Cleveland Hills almost to the sea. Perchance these moors are most lovely in their September garb of purple heather, but whenever the sunlight touches the wooded dells and rapid streams of the dales, or brightens the lonely heights, there is always an unending pageant of rugged, natural beauty. Here the work of Nature is the main thing; villages and habitations, which are few in number and stone-built, blend into the scene and are but secondary factors of it. Most of the cross-roads are rough, and they

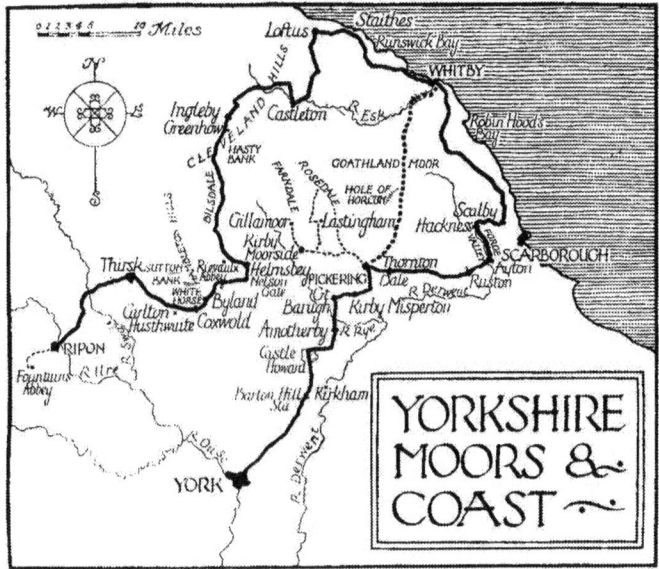

twist and turn up and down hills; between them are trackways and moorland walks. To the north-east of the moors are the little fishing villages of the coast, while to the south are the rich lands of the Plain of York.

York, busy enough in these days with peaceful pursuits, still bears the panoply of war. The grey old walls, studded with towers and turrets and posterns, link continuously past with present, and the four great gates tell of the hopes and ambitions of generations that have passed. For York was always the chief city of the North; it has been connected with some of the most thrilling chapters of English history, and round its existing defences, as well as those of earlier times, many military dramas have been enacted. The fortifications, remaining much as they were when the Wars of the Roses were fought, are therefore no ordinary spectacle. Within the walls the architectural gem, of course, is the Minster; there also are churches, old buildings, and houses, to recall the bygone city that was a centre of ecclesiasticism, a home of monks, and where nobles such as the Percys, and squires too, gathered in mediæval and later days. The quiet courtyard of St. William's College, the gabled King's Manor in which James I and Charles I both stayed, the the Treasurer's House that was reconstructed about the year 1620, and the narrow street called Shambles, with houses overhanging and almost meeting at the upper storeys, are all excellent reminders of the city's past.

Not far from the three great towers of the Cathedral will be found the road for Malton. It passes through pastoral country, level at first, but later broken by undulations. After Barton Hill station is reached—the Norman ruins of Kirkham Priory lie in a delicious valley of the Derwent three miles to the east—a left-hand turning goes over hills and through the finely-wooded park of Castle Howard. The mansion is one of the very great houses of England, erected by Vanbrugh at the beginning of the eighteenth century. Like Blenheim, and other notable buildings of that time, it testifies to the splendour and magnificence that was the aim of wealthy noblemen when George I was king. To the right, at the end of the park, is Coneysthorpe, elevated land, and a descent into the wide vale at Amotherby. The Kirby Moorside road is followed to Great Barugh. Here a branch goes by Kirby Misperton to the church spire, castle ruins, and winding streets of the pretty little town of Pickering. Standing amidst the rounded hills, woods, and steepish valleys that mark the southern boundary of the north-east Yorkshire moors, it is the centre of a number of ways that lead to much picturesque scenery, notably one running north to the Hole of Horcum and Goathland Moor, and one, turning west, to Kirky Moorside, Lastingham, Gillamoor, Rosedale and Farndale. From Pickering the route continues by an easy road, under green slopes, through Thornton Dale and the small stone village of Ruston. Near to the bridge and the somewhat insignificant remains of the castle at Ayton, a left turning, for Hackness, traverses the narrow and deep Forge Valley, watered by a quick stream rippling beneath exposed rocks and hanging woods. This lovely road, after winding by Hackness Church and Hall, mounts

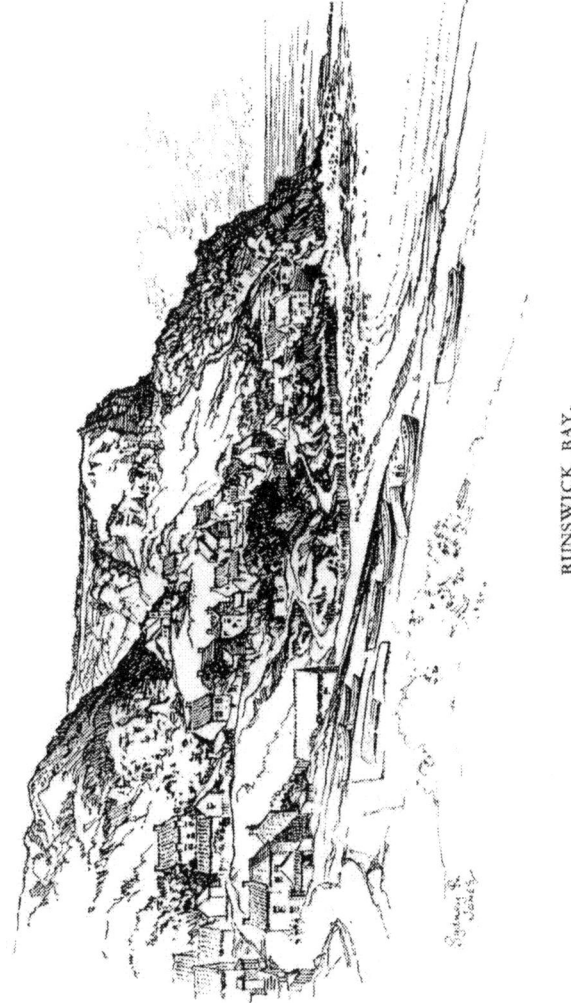

RUNSWICK BAY.

steadily through Hackness Park. At the crest of the hill is the first glimpse of the sea and Scarborough Castle crowning a great promontory.

Scalby, the next village, is on the highway that runs by moor and sea to Whitby and Loftus. Throughout this length of road side ways lead to the cliffs and the little places on the shore, so often pictured on the walls of the Royal Academy. There are many notable scenes—the graceful lines of the bays of Robin Hood and Runswick, Whitby's

RIEVAULX BANK.

Abbey and steep town of bright roofs, and such quaint fishing villages as Robin Hood's Town, Runswick and Staithes.

At Loftus is the turning for the Cleveland dales and moors, the valley of the Esk, Castleton, and the road between the hills to Ingleby Greenhow. Then follows the sharp ascent of Hasty Bank which leads down through the high slopes of Bilsdale. At the end of the dale, and near to the foot of a dangerous hill, a sharp turn quite suddenly reveals a vision of Gothic beauty and green enchantment. Lying low in a secluded spot, a veritable Eden, stands Rievaulx, most exquisite of abbeys. Three miles on is the pretty open

PLATE XIX.

BILSDALE.

HEATHER ON THE HAMBLETON HILLS.

THE "WHITE HORSE," KILBURN.

PLATE XX.

BARDEN TOWER, WHARFEDALE.

TROUGH OF BOWLAND.

LEE AND LITTLEDALE FELL.

square of Helmsley, situated below a double line of earthworks that encircle Buckingham's Castle built round an ancient keep.

Over the bridge by the York road as far as Nelson Gate, Duncombe Park, and by the right-hand way for Thirsk, is a long climb up to the heather and open moors of the Hambleton Hills. Here the Coxwold road diverges to the left down a long, steep hill. It is enclosed by plantations that frame, near the end of the descent, a prospect of Byland Abbey, lonely and ruined. Not far away lies the trim street of Coxwold village, completed by a proper rural group of old cottages, church, and inn. Shandy Hall, beyond the church, and the timbered house at Carlton Husthwaite, three miles distant, are both good examples of old domestic architecture. All the way into Thirsk the rugged spurs of the Hambleton Hills break away to the east; they include Sutton Bank, a celebrated hill-climb for motorists, and the White Horse of Kilburn, cut on the face of a slope. Across the valley from Thirsk stands the great tower of Ripon Cathedral; below it the old streets are full of charm, and there is a fine large Market Place. It is but three more miles to that marvellous pile, Fountains Abbey, most rare and beautiful in its setting of water and trees.

ROUTE 18

A LENGTH of good road passes over York plain and rises into Knaresborough. Although pleasant enough the way is uneventful, but the country hereabout was once much connected with the course of English history. To the south, and reached by the turning at Marston Station, is the fateful ground of Marston Moor, where Prince Rupert, greatly daring after his brilliant manœuvre into York, engaged his army with the Parliamentary troops on July 2, 1644; when darkness came the Royalist forces were shattered, and, wrote Cromwell after the fight, " God made them as stubble to our swords." There are memories of Cromwell and Fairfax, too, at Knaresborough, Ripley, and other places nearby. West of Marston the road crosses the river Nidd and, short

of Knaresborough, passes near to Goldsborough Hall, a brick and stone house built in 1620, and now the home of Princess Mary, Viscountess Lascelles.

The Castle at Knaresborough, which was granted in 1371 to John of Gaunt, though it existed long before his time, has lain in ruins since the days of the Civil War. The old Manor House, visited by Cromwell about the date of the Preston fight, is an interesting gabled structure, containing old panelling and a fireplace of the seventeenth century. The town is a place for views, one of the best being obtained from the riverside, where the houses are seen piling up to the Castle that crowns a rocky eminence — a capital subject for canvas or camera. In a few miles Ripley and its Castle are reached, where a left turning goes through Killinghall, and by the

YORK TO LANCASTER

Lindley reservoir and Farnley Park, to Otley. On this road the hills begin. They extend westwards right across Yorkshire into Lancashire, and include some of the heights of the Pennine Chain. This tract of country throughout is impressive; it contains famous river valleys, often clothed in trees, waterfalls, becks and likely places for trout, great wide moors, and fells and high mountains where

KNARESBOROUGH.

the air is pure and fine. Here and there are notable ruins, while the best examples of the old and characterful Yorkshire houses—usually built of the local millstone grit—are dotted up and down the hillsides. There is little wonder that this region has appealed to both literary and artistic minds. Wordsworth found inspiration in Wharfedale, Turner's frequent visits to Farnley Hall prompted a wonderful series of paintings from his master hand, and the genius of the Brontë sisters was greatly influenced by the surroundings of their Haworth home. Lines in *The White Doe of Rylstone*, passages in *Wuthering Heights* and *Shirley*, and Turner's works that hang at Farnley, all vividly and delicately sum up the fascination and meaning of these romantic Yorkshire lands. Almost every road through them is hilly, except where the levels of the rivers are touched. The smaller roads, on which very steep climbs and descents are encountered, are almost all practicable for wheeled traffic, though the surfaces on the higher elevations are rough and loose. The London-Edinburgh motor run includes the valley of the Wharfe and, in 1926, followed the mountain way that leads over into Hawes and Wensley Dale. For

CLITHEROE.

those who walk, the whole district between the Wharfe and the Ribble is remarkably attractive.

From the bridge, and the grey stone walls and roofs of Otley town, are two ways up the Wharfe valley to Bolton Bridge, one by the north bank of the river, and one by the south. The former is the prettier and least frequented, so it is best to stop short at Otley bridge, turn right, and follow the left-hand route for Weston, Denton Park, the outskirts of Ilkley, the hillside hamlet of Nesfield, and thus reach Bolton Bridge This narrow, but quite good, road gives many fine glimpses of river and hilly scenery, dóminated by the impressive mass of Rumbles Moor; it also goes near the old Grammar School in Otley, the Elizabethan hall and mediæval tithe-barn at Weston, and the old bridge of Ilkley, while Middleton Lodge, of the seventeenth century, lies high on a hill to the north.

At Bolton Bridge the turning by the hotel leads to the Abbey, and the beautiful reaches of the upper Wharfe. The graceful scene of woods and flowing waters, overhung by mountains and moors, extends all the way to Burnsall ; it is enriched in turn by Bolton's " pile of state, overthrown and desolate," and by the ruins of Barden Tower, where lived the studious Lord Clifford, in youth banished as a shepherd through his father's deeds in the Wars of the Roses, and in late manhood a hero of Flodden Field. Further up the valley is the walker's country over and around Great Whernside and Nidderdale. The turning at Threshfield, however, gives plenty of up and down work right into Gargrave. This village is on a main highway. At Skipton, to the left, is an impressive group of church and castle ; in front, beyond Settle, are the high mountains that rise above rugged hamlets and old halls such as Lawkland, Clapdale, and Newby.

PACKHORSE BRIDGE, MYTTON GREEN.

From Gargrave to West Marton, and by a long hill down into the attractive street of Gisburn, leads into the Ribble valley, which in many ways compares with that of the Wharfe. Bolton by Bowland, with a cross and stocks on the green, Downham, Pendle Hill, Harrop Fell, and other places hereabout are well worth seeing. Clitheroe, the near town, is chiefly notable for its Castle ruins ; when the right-hand turning (the Whitewell road) is taken as far as "Eddisford Bridge Inn," and the left branch for Mytton there followed, the Castle and town are seen standing finely amidst the surrounding hills. There are many points of interest in this vicinity. Bashall Hall, beyond the inn, shows a good bay window ; Mytton Green, when gained, appeals by its old stonework, and by its situation, overlooking a broad sweep of the Ribble ; the pack-horse bridge in the wooded Hodder valley, standing parallel to the Longridge road and connecting the counties of York and Lancaster, makes a particularly graceful span over the water; and, after leaving Stoneyhurst College and Hurst Green, the left turning, for Ribchester, carries past Dutton Hall—a capital example of an old Lancashire house—and drops down to the "White Bull," stone cottages, and cobbled streets of Ribchester, once a station of the Romans. Many interesting Roman finds can be seen in the museum by the church.

By ascending to Longridge, and passing through Whitewell, a turn to the left mounts up the narrow and impressive Trough of Bowland. This lonely way is rough and steep. After the county boundary stone has been passed, it winds down between fir trees into Lancashire and, bordered by moor and stream, reaches Lee and Appletree, and eventually ends in Lancaster town.

ROUTE 19

LANCASTER, old before John of Gaunt knew it, stands in pastoral country, between the sea and the rocks of the Pennine Chain. North of the town, the lanes around Nether Kellet command splendid views of Morecambe Bay, which glistens with stretches of golden sand when the tide is out. Inland, the River Lune winds through sylvan scenes, and in its valley are old churches and villages. Here are stone-built houses and cottages, somewhat gaunt in appearance, but distinguished by the panelled and dated headstones of their doorways. Such buildings are numerous at Halton and Caton, as well as in Lancaster. East of Lancaster, on the far side of the luxuriant lowlands, are the fells and dales of Yorkshire.

The heights are approached from Lancaster by the road following the south side of the river. Claughton's old towers, set with many mullions, are first neared, and then Thurland Castle is reached. The main road and the river continue northward, where, in the words of Ruskin, "the valley of the Lune at Kirby is one of the loveliest scenes in England—therefore, in the world. Whatever moorland hill, and sweet river, and English forest foliage can be at their best, is

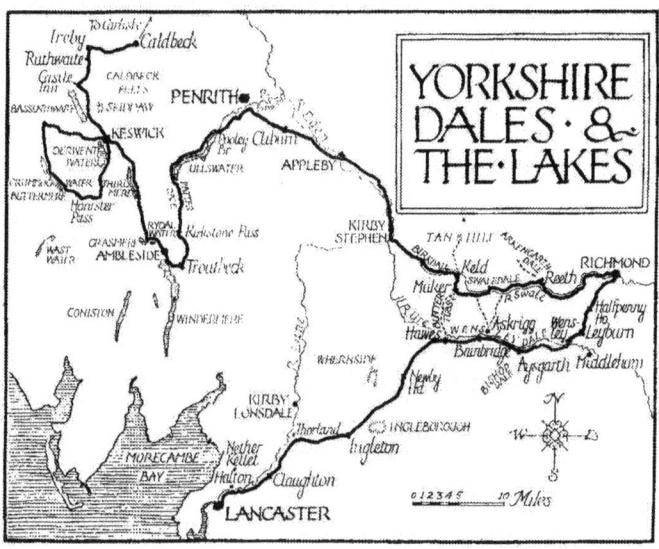

gathered there." Branching to the right at Thurland, for Burton in Lonsdale, Ingleton, Ribble Head, and Hawes, the tourist leaves behind the fresh green of the lowlands and penetrates into high, rugged places. The mountains are grand and solitary, and stone crops out from their sides; below them, the wild beauty of the dales and the plunging waters of rapid rivers and streams are ever alluring. Up in this fine, open country, where the winters are long and severe, the true dalesmen live and tend their sheep.

Mounting up from Ingleton to Hawes gives a fitting introduction to the West Yorkshire scene. Whernside and Ingleborough rise on the left and right, Dale Beck runs by the roadside, and the moors at Newby Head reach over 1,400 feet. The road, having ascents of 1 in 10-15, is typical of others in the locality, and all those who explore the dales must be prepared for steep gradients, twists and turns, and narrow, rough ways. Motorists will find plenty of tests for skilful driving; for those who walk, there are unfrequented routes through mountain splendour in every direction. Hawes is in Wensleydale. Over the river is the Butter Tubs Pass, impressive and wild, giving formidable climbs into Swaledale. Eastwards, keeping to the south side of the Ure, are Bainbridge and Aysgarth. Askrigg, a grey little town, can be reached by the bridge at Worton; it has a gabled hall, of 1678, overlooking the bull ring, and the embattled towers of Nappa Hall are a mile away. Beyond the town, two routes over high country into Swaledale, both practicable

BAINBRIDGE, WENSLEYDALE.

for motors, diverge to the right and left. Past Aysgarth, where the river comes down in a series of rapids, Bishopdale opens out, giving uninterrupted communication to Wharfedale. Fine scenery, now enriched with greenery and trees, continues to Wensley and Leyburn. On the far side of the valley the great fortress-mansion of Bolton Castle breaks the sky-line, while the massive, twelfth-century keep of Middleham stands away to the south. At Halfpenny House, three miles from Leyburn, the turning to the right gives more stiff climbs, but magnificent views, before reaching the ancient town of Richmond.

Richmond Castle with the bridge and river, forming a group that has been painted and drawn by countless artists,

THE LAKES

is one of the sights of England. Swaledale, running eastwards up to the mountains, is no less impressive than Wensleydale. It is served by a good road that gradually mounts up to Reeth through splendid open scenery. Arkengarthdale, to the right from Reeth, though more wild and bleak, gives a capital run up to the moor. Higher up the Swale is Muker, a village nestling below fine heights. Here the river, forsaking the road, is seen tracing its way through the dale. Further on, a sharp turn to the left shews the end of the Butter Tubs

MIDDLEHAM CASTLE, NEAR LEYBURN.

Pass. From Thwaite to Keld a mountain route commences, giving a right-hand branch at Keld—with surface rough, and hairpin bends—for Tan Hill and wonderful panoramas. Onward through Birkdale means much hard climbing, but ample rewards lie in the beauty of mountain torrents, the great distances, and the exhilaration that comes with the rise to high altitudes. A long drop of four miles, with gradients of 1 in 8, leads to Kirby Stephen and the lovely valley of the Eden.

The well-known touring country of Lakeland lies ahead. It may be approached through Appleby by here crossing the Eden for Cliburn and the Penrith road. Short of Penrith, the River Eamont is followed to Pooley Bridge, a gateway to scenes of broad waters, woodlands, and magnificent mountains, unmatched elsewhere in the length and breadth of England. The road by the banks of Ullswater reaches Patterdale, Brothers' Water, and the precipitous Kirkstone Pass, familiar to hill-climbing motorists. After Troutbeck comes the right-hand turning by Windermere for Ambleside, Rydal Water, and Grasmere, in the heart of Wordsworth's Lakeland. Here, also, the Coleridges lived (Nab Cottage is quite near to Rydal Mount), and down by the waters of Coniston, in sight of a wonderful prospect, is John Ruskin's home. Thirlmere, next skirted, is on the way to Keswick, where Skiddaw rises grandly over the town. The circular route from Keswick, embracing Derwentwater, Buttermere, and Crummock Water, is one of exceptional beauty, but after an easy run of seven miles, Honister Pass, together with other formidable hills, must be faced. Those who wish to wander further from Keswick can explore the haunts of John Peel—up amongst the Caldbeck Fells—by taking the Carlisle highway to "Castle Inn," where the right-hand turning at the cross-roads is followed for Ruthwaite, a hamlet to the south of Ireby in sight of the heights and open country that the huntsman knew so well. John Peel's home at Ruthwaite is a modest stone dwelling, and his famous horn, no longer "far, far away," now hangs in the "Sun Inn" at Ireby; in Caldbeck churchyard, to be reached by a heathery, moorland way, the stone that bears his name can be seen. Carlisle, and the Roman Wall, lie not many miles to the north.

ROUTE 20

CARLISLE, so often called the "merry city," rejoices in a singularly full record of strife, well coloured with fights, sacks, hangings, and burnings! A mere catalogue of the troubles the town has passed through, from the dawn of its history down to the lively days of 1745, would fill pages. Its geographical position, close to the Border, no doubt accounted for much. Parts of the Castle built by William Rufus, remain and on the western side of the city some of

PLATE XXI.

MARSKE, SWALEDALE.

CRUMMOCK WATER.

PLATE XXII.

THE GREEN, ELSDON.

ROTHBURY AND SIMONSIDE

THE ROMAN WALL 123

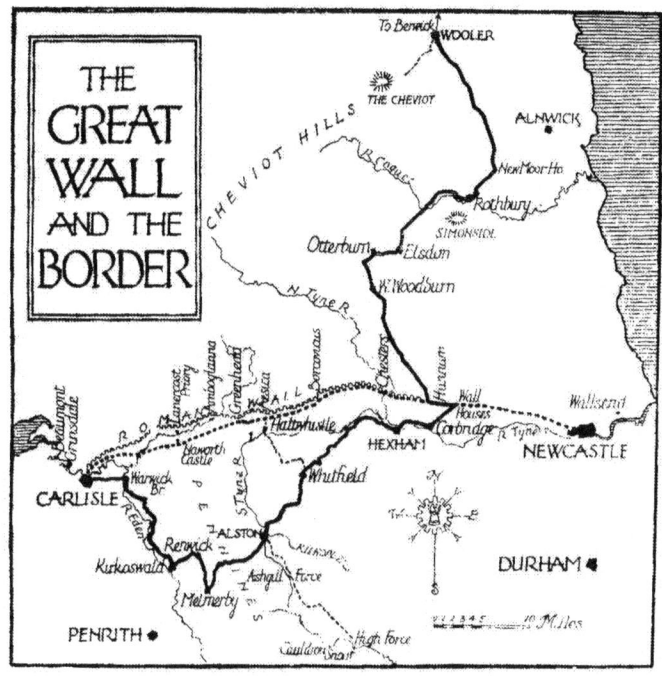

the walls erected by Henry I still stand. Cromwell's contributions to the misfortunes of Carlisle were significant and characteristic; he partly demolished the very beautiful Cathedral, but fortunately spared the choir with its magnificent east window.

Carlisle, however, was concerned with one chapter of Border warfare which, above all others, stirs the imagination. It was a station on the Great Wall. Of the many relics that recall the days of Roman Britain, none is quite so inspiring as Hadrian's Wall, built from sea to sea, from Solway Firth to Wallsend on the Tyne. Wellnigh indestructible, it remains the grandest monument in the country of the power and indomitable purpose of the rulers of the Roman Empire. It had its beginnings with Agricola. This governor, about

A.D. 79, constructed a series of forts, connected by a military road, on the Carlisle-Newcastle line, to keep back the incursions of the warlike people of Scotland. Time proved these defences to be inadequate; the forts were lost, and whole cohorts of Roman soldiers were utterly destroyed by the invaders. Then came the Emperor Hadrian, a distinguished general and a great builder. Leaving Rome to travel throughout his empire, he appears to have reached England in A.D. 122. He turned his attention to the north, and to him is generally ascribed the repair and consolidation of the northern boundary of the Province of Britain. New forts were built a little to the north of Agricola's road, the ditch, or Vallum, was made, and finally the Great Wall came into being.

The large forts of Hadrian's bulwark, situated several miles apart, contained the quarters for commanders and men, and places for all necessary stores. They were connected by the Wall, which had average dimensions of about eight feet wide and twenty feet high. In front of it was a V-shaped ditch; on its southern side ran the military way and the Vallum. Between the large forts were smaller forts, or milecastles, placed at regular intervals of roughly a mile, and the rampart-walk of the Wall, furnished with turrets to serve as sentry-boxes, joined every fort and mile-castle. Such was the system of the Roman defence, from which watch was kept unceasingly. So great in conception was the work, and so solidly was it constructed, that there are few places at which it has been wholly lost since the legions returned to Rome.

Although little of the Wall remains at Carlisle, much of it is to be seen near by. In the west, it can be traced at Grinsdale, and from Beaumont Church to Burgh. To the east, the Wall can be followed for miles. From Tarraby it runs through pleasant country, in sight of blue hills and watered by the Rivers Eden and Irthing, right up to Lanercost Priory, a beautiful ruin built of Roman stones, and containing Roman altars. To the south of the river is the feudal fortress of Naworth, one of the numberless strongholds with which this once turbulent district was studded. Further on, the Wall mounts below Banks Fell to Amboglanna, the largest of the forts. From here it continues its course, rising over

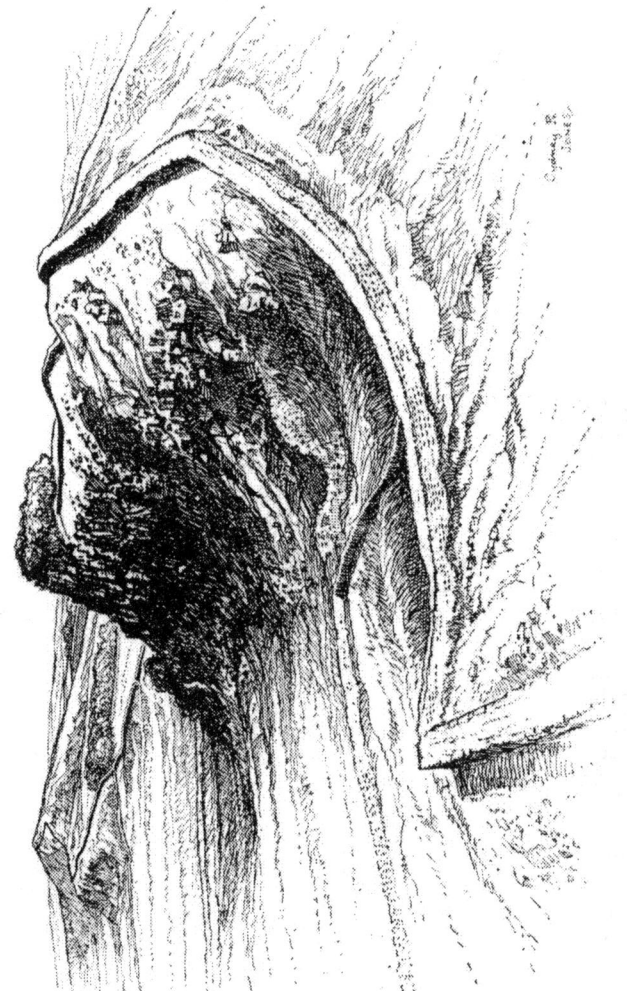

THE ROMAN WALL AT CUDDY'S CRAG, NEAR BORCOVICUS.

hills, descending into glens, and sometimes clinging to rocks. In this wild moorland country, whose silence is broken only by the sounds of the winds and the sheep and the curlews, and where the Cheviot Hills shew in the far-off distance, are the remains of the forts of Æsica and Borcovicus, with Vindolana lying a little back to the south. Some miles to the east, in the valley of the North Tyne, are the excavations of Cilurnum, the fine museum of Chesters, and the abutments of the bridge that carried the Wall over the river. From the highway connecting Carlisle and Newcastle every part of the Wall can be reached. For many miles the modern road hugs the line of the Wall and the Vallum, but the most romantic section, between Greenhead and Housesteads (Borcovicus), and parts nearer to Carlisle, can only be explored on foot.

Starting from Carlisle, away from the Roman wall and by the road south of the river, a pretty way from Warwick Bridge leads up the Eden valley to Kirkoswald. After turning to the left for Renwick, and to the right for Melmerby, prepare for real mountain scenery and real mountain climbs. Up among the Pennines it is wild and bleak. The expanses of the moors and fells are vast, but the passes are wonderful and the views magnificent. Where the rivers come down from the heights, waterfalls leap over rugged rocks. From Melmerby, a hill of almost five miles is followed by an equally long drop into Alston, the highest market town in England. This is in the centre of a district notable for waterfalls and passes. The most impressive falls are Nent Force, near the confluence of the Rivers Nent and South Tyne, Ashgill Force, and in Teesdale, Cauldron Snout, and the best waterfall in England, known as High Force. The Ashgill pass is one of the finest moorland passes in the whole country. The Hartside pass from Melmerby to Alston and from Alston to Whitfield has a zigzag of about twenty miles. Mounting to an altitude of over 1,500 feet, a long descent succeeds, down to the lower lands of Whitfield. Over the slopes of Whitfield Moor, a left-hand road goes to Haltwhistle and the Great Wall.

Straight ahead, the route continues through the Border country of song and story, where many ruins and peel-towers

THE BORDER

tell of the days of moss-troopers and thieves, and marauders who swept down from Scotland. After Staward Peel and Langley Castle comes the wooded valley of the South Tyne, sheltering historic Hexham and Corbridge, the great centre for Roman soldiers proceeding to and from the military base at York. North-east, at Wall Houses, General Wade's road of 1753, keeping to the line of the Wall, gains the crest of Stagshaw Bank. Here the right-hand turning—the Roman road into Scotland—switchbacks through lonely, desolate country, where hills recede far away into the distance. Three

KILLHOPE PASS, NEAR ALSTON.
THE HIGHEST PASS IN ENGLAND—2,056 FEET.

miles past the river at West Woodburn is a way to the right for Otterburn, scene of the battle between Douglas and Hotspur, which lives in the ballad of *The Battle of Otterbourne*.

Elsdon, with a spacious green and a rectory fortified against the raids of the cattle-stealers, will be seen before climbing the hill that leads into the valley of the Coquet, where Rothbury stands in an exceptionally beautiful position. This place has great attractions. In Cragside, it possesses a Norman Shaw house and wonderful gardens. To the south rise the crags and heathery slopes of Simonside, while away to the north-west are blue hills. Down by the riverside, on sunshiny days, the views are remarkably fine, as the clouds, travelling fast, throw moving shadows across expanses of brown moor and heather.

Another upward pull must be faced from Rothbury to New Moor House, where the undulating road—pretty, but generally windy—goes northward to Wooler, leaving Alnwick Castle to the east. Here at Wooler, in reach of the humpy grass hills of the Cheviots that give wide panoramic views, this route ends. If the traveller wishes to gain the Cheviot itself, he can drive or ride along the rough road by the Harthope Burn for about five miles, but the final ascent must perforce be made on foot. In numberless points round about, and all the way down to Carlisle, names and places—Homildon Hill, Flodden, Yeavering, and many another—constantly recall the older Border warfare that inspired so much of the poetry of this land of ballad and song.

INDEX

N.B.—*The figures in heavy type indicate illustrations in the text.*

Abberton, 22
Abbes Roding, 18
Abbey Dore, 68
Abbot's Bromley, 72
Abingdon, 57, 60
Abinger, 11
Ackling Dyke, 32
Acle, 95
Aisthorpe Valley, **102**
Albury, 12
Alfoxton, 43, 44
Alnwick, 108
Alport, 79
Alston, 126
Alton, 4, 13
Amberley Castle, 122
Ambleside, 122
Amesbury, 29, 32
Amotherby, 110
Amwell Hill, 27
Andover, xiv, 29
Appleby, 121
Arden, 55
Ardleigh, 20
Arminghall, 90
Armitage, 72
Arthur's Castle, 50
Arun, the, 2
Arundel, 3
Arundel Castle, 16
Ashbourne, 57
Ashburton, 46
Ashby, 56
Ashdown Forest, 16
Ashen, 19
Ashford, 79
Ashgill Force, 126
Ashow, 65
Ashridge Park, 26
Ashton, 66

Ashwell, 26
Asser, ix
Asthall Manor, 63
Aston Hall, 24
Atherington, 44
Audley End, 19
Avebury, 34 ; earthworks, **35**
Avon, river and valley, 31, 33, 55, 63
Avon, the, at Middle Woodford, Plate VII
Avon, the Bristol, 29
Axminster, 29
Aylsham, 93, 94
Ayot Green, 27
Aysgarth, 120
Ayton, 110

Badbury Rings, 31
Bag Enderby, 104
Bainbridge, **120**
Bakewell, 57, 79
Balcombe Forest, 16
Baldock, 26
Bamburgh, 108
Banbury, 56
Barden Tower, 117
Bardon Hill, 66
Barford, 65
Barley, 26
Barnet, 3
Barnham Broom, 91
Barnstaple, 44
Barrington, 33
Barrow, 71
Barrowdene, Plate XI
Barton, 26
Baslow, 80
Bath, 3, 32, 33, 38
Bath Road, the, 29, 33, 54

129

Beacon Hill, 71
Beaminster, 32
Beaudesert, 72
Beaulieu, 38
Beckford, 66
Beckhampton Green, 34
Beckley, 60
Bedford Rivers, Old and New, 96
Bedhampton, 14
Beeding, 16
Beer Head, Seaton, Plate VII
Begby, 102
Belton Park, 100
Belvoir, 70
Bere, 2
Bere Regis, 37
Berkhampstead, 26
Berry Pomeroy Castle, 48
Berwick, 106
Beverley, 108
Bicton, 75
Bideford, 44
Bidford, 66
Bidford Bridge, 56
Bignor, 2, 16
Bildeston, 88
Bilsdale, 112, Plate XIX
Binham Abbey, 92
Binton Bridge, 66
Bird's Green, **18**
Birkdale, 121
Birkland Forest, 81, Plate XIV
Birts Morton, 57, 67
Bisham, 23
Bishops Canning, 36
Bishop's Castle, 74
Bishops Lydeard, 43
Bishops Waltham, 4
Black Country, the, 55, map **70**
Black Mountains, 68, 75
Blackdown Hills, 30
Blackmoor Vale, 37
Blackwater, the, 22
Blakeney, 93
" Blakesmoor," 26, 27
Blandford, 30, 32, 37
Blickling, 93
Blofield, 95
Bodiam Castle, 4, 6
Bodmin Moor, 30, 49

Bolton, 108, 116, 117
Bolton Castle, 120
Border, the, map **123**
Boroughbridge, 107
Boscastle, 50
Boscobel House, 72
Boston, 82, 84, **104**
Boulter's Lock, 23
Bourton-on-the-Water, 63
Bow Beach, 4
Bowland, Trough of, 118, Plate XX
Boxted, 20
Brackley, 57, 60
Bradford, 107
Bradford-on-Avon, 39
Bradgate, 71
Bramber, 16
Bray, 23
Bredon Hill, 64, 66, **67**
Brent Eleigh, 88, Plate XV
Bricklehampton, 66
Bridgnorth, 57
Bridlington, 107
Brigg, 102
Brighton, 3
Bristol Channel, Plate I
Brixham, 32, 48
Broads, the, 83, map **90**
Broadway, xvii, 66
Brocket, 27
Brockhall, 55
Bromyard, 67
Brooke, 90
Broom, 66
Brothers' Water, 122
Broughton Hill, 70
Brown Clee Hill, 74
Brown Willy, 49
Brownhills, 72
Bubbenhall, 65
Buckfastleigh, 47
Budby, 81
Bude, 50
Buildwas Abbey, 74
Bungay, 90
Bure, the, 93, 94
Burford, 57, 62, 63
Burham, 10, Plate III
Burton in Lonsdale, 119

INDEX

Bury St. Edmunds, 82, 86
Buttermere, 106, 122

Caldbeck Fells, 122
Cambridge, 82, 95
Cammas Hall, 18
Cannock, 72
Cannock Chase, 72, **73**
Canons Ashby, 59
Canterbury, 3, 8, 10
Capek, Karel, x
Carlisle, 106, 108, 122, 123
Carlton Husthwaite, 113
Castle Howard, 110
Castle Rising, 83, 100
Castleton, 79, 112
Caton, 118
Caythorpe, 100
Chagford, 47, Plate IX
Chanctonbury Ring, 16
Chard, 41
Charnwood, 55, 71
Charnwood Forest, Plate XIII
Chatsworth, 80
Chelsworth, 88
Chesham, 4, 26
Cheshire, route map, **76**
Chester, 57, 77
Chesterfield, 80
Cheviots, the, 107, 120
Chichester, 2
Chiddingstone, 4, 5
Chideock, 42
Childrey, 62
Chilterns, the, xvii, 1, 2, map **23**, 24, **25**
Chinnor, 24
Chipping Campden, 57, 66
Church Stretton, 74, Plate XIII
Cirencester, 56, 57, 62, 63
Clapdale, 117
Clare, 4, 19
Claughton, 118
Clavering, 26, Plate VI
Cleveland Hills, 108, 112
Clewer, 22
Cley, 93
Cliburn, 121
Clifford Castle, 68
Clifton Campville, 72

Cilfton Hampden, 60
Clifton Maybank, 33
Clitheroe, **116**, 117
Clivedon Reach, 23
Clun Valley, xiii, 75
Cobham, 21
Cocking, 14
Cocksfield, 87
Codford, 36
Colchester, 2, 20, 22
Coldharbour, 11, Plate IV
Coleby, 100
Coln, the, 62
Coltishall Broad, Plate II
Colville Hall, 18
Compton Winyates, 57, 66
Coneysthorpe, 110
Congleton, 79
Coniston, 122
Constable Country, the, map **17**
Cookham, 23
Corbridge, 127
Corfe Castle, 38
Cornwall, map **49**
Cornish Headlands, Plate X
Corsham, 32, 39
Corve Dale, 74
Cothelstone, 42, 43
Cotswolds, the, xvii, 54, 56, 57, map **58**, 62
Coventry, xiii, 56
Cowbie, **99**
Cowdray Castle, 14
Coxwold Road, 113
Crackington Cove, 50
Cradley, 67, Plate XII
Cragside, 127
Cranborne, 32
Cranborne Chase, 30
Craven Arms, 74
Crewkerne, 41
Crockenwell, 47
Cromer, 82, 83
Cropthorne, 66
Cross Keys, 99, 100
Crowborough, 16
Crowland, 98
Crummock Water, 122, Plate XXI
Cubert, 51

K*

INDEX

Dagnal, 26
Dale Beck, 119
Dane Hill, 16
Darlington, 106
Dartmoor, 30, 31, 45, 46
Dartmouth, 32, 47
Deal, 8
Dean, Forest of, 55
Debenham, **88**, 89
Dedham, 20, **21**
Deeping Fen, **98**
Delamere, 55
Derbyshire Dales, 54
Derwent, the, 55, 107, 110
Derwentwater, 122
Desford Old Hall, 71
Devil's Dyke, 16
Devizes Green, 36
Dinton, 37
Ditchling, 16
Dittisham, 47
Doone Valley, 44
Dorchester, 29
Dorking, 11
Doulting, 40
Dove, the, 55, 72
Dove Dale, 79, **80**
Downs, xiii, xvii, 1, 16
Downs, South, **xi**, **12**
Downs and the Weald, **15**
Dukeries, the, map **76**, 80
Dulcot Hill, 40
Dulverton, 44
Duncombe Park, 113
Dunmow, 17
Dunstable, 3, 26
Dunster, 32, 44, Plate I
Durham, 108
Dutton Hall, 118

Eamont, the, 121
Eardisland, 67
East Barsham, 91
East Barsham Hall, 84
East Bergholt, 20
East Dereham, 91
East Grinstead, 16
East Hagbourne, 60, Plate XI
East Holland, 105
East Knoyle, 37

East Tisted, 14
Eastwood, 38
Edburton, 16
Eden, the, 107, 121, 126
Edge Hill, 56, 65
Edington, 36
Edwinstowe, 81, Plate XIV
Elsdon, 127, the Green, Plate XXII
Elsenham, 19
Elsick, 74
England, general map of, Plate VIII
Epping Forest, 2, 17
Erlestoke, 36
Ermine Street, xii, 3, 83, 102
Esk, valley of the, 112
Essex, map **17**
Euston Park, 89
Evesham, Vale of, 55, 56, 66, **67**
Exe, valley of the, 44
Exeter, 29, 45, 46
Exhall, 66
Exmoor, 30, 31

Fairford, 62
Fairleigh, 39
Fairleigh Hungerford, 38
Fakenham, 91
Falmouth, 52
Fareham Road, 14
Farndale, 110
Farnham, 4, 13
Farnley Park, 115
Felsham, 87
Fenny Stratford, 56
Fens, the, 82, 83, 84, 95, map **96**, 97
Filey, 107
Fillingham, 102
Finchingfield, 19
Fingest, 24
Flempton, 86
Floore, 59
Florden, 91
Fordwich, 8, Plate III
Forest Row, 16
Forge Valley, 110
Fosse Way, 29, 32, 56, 71, 83
Fountains Abbey, 108, 113

INDEX

Fowey, 32, 53
Framlingham, 89
Fritwell, 60
Frome, 38, 40
Funtington, 14
Fyfield, 33

Gargrave, 117
Gawsworth Hall, 78, **78**
Gedding Hall, 84, 87
Geddington, 59
Gedney Marshes, 99
Geological formations, xvii, general map showing, **xviii**, 2, 30, 82, 106, 107
Glastonbury, 32, 40
Glentworth, 102
Gloucester, 56
Goathland Moor, 110
Golden Valley, 68
Golsborough Hall, 114
Gopsal Hall, 72
Goudhurst, 6
Grafton, 66
Grantham, 82, 100
Great Bardfield, 19
Great Bartlow, Plate V
Great Barugh, 110
Great Brington, 59
Great Chalfield, 39
Great Cheverell, 36
Great North Road, 82
Great Snoring, 91, **92**
Great Whernside, 117
Greenhead, 126
Gretton, 58
Grimsby, 82
Grindleford Bridge, 80
Groby, 71
Groombridge, 5
Grovely Wood, 32
Guildford, 12
Guist, 91
Guy's Cliff Mill, 65

Hackness, 110
Haddon, xiii, 57, 79
Hadham Market, 87
Halton, 118
Halton Holegate, 105

Haltwhistle, 126
Hambledon Lock, 24, Plate VI
Hambleton Hills, 108, Plate XIX, 113
Hanbury, 72
Handforth, 78
Harbledown, 10
Hardwick House, 86
Hartfield, Ashdown Forest, Plate IV
Hartington, 79
Harwell, 60
Haslemere, 2
Hasty Bank, 112
Hathersage, 80
Hawes, 116, 119, 120
Hawkhurst, 6
Haworth, 115
Hay, 57, 67, 68
Hay Tor, 47
Helmsley, 113
Helston, 52
Helvellyn, 107
Hengistbury Head, 31
Hengrave Hall, 86
Henham, 19
Henley-in-Arden, xii
Hennacliff, 50
Hereford, 56
Hertford, 27
Hessenford, 53
Hexham, 127
Heytesbury, 36
Hickling Broad, xiii, 95, Plate XVI
High Toynton, 104
High Wycombe, 4
Highwayside, 78
Hillborough, 66
Hinton St. George, 41, **42**
Hobhole Drain, 105
Hog's Back, 12
Holbeach, 99
Holkham, 100
Hollybush, 67
Holmbury Hill, 11
Holt, 93
Holton Beckering, 104
Holywell, **xx**, 96
Homildon Hill, 128

INDEX

Honister Pass, 106, 122
Horncastle waterway, Plate XVIII
Horner, 44, **45**
Horsted Keynes, 16
Houghton Bridge, 16
Houghton Regis, 26
Hoveton, 94
Hungerford, 33, 39
Hunstanton, 83
Hurst Green, 118
Hythe, 8

Ibetstone Green, 24
Ibstone, 24
Ickham, 8
Icklington, 83
Icknield Way, 24, 26, 83
Ilchester, 29, 41
Ilkley, 106, 116
Ilminster, 41
Ingham, 87
Ingleborough, 119
Ingleby Greenhow, 112
Ingleton, 119
Ipswich, 82, 86, 89
Irby, 105
Irvinghoe Beacon, 24
Ivybridge, 46
Ixworth, 87

Keld, 121
Kenilworth, 56, 65
Kennet, the, 33
Keswick, 122
Kilburn, "White Horse," at, 113, Plate XIX
Killhope Pass, **107**
Kilpeck, 68
Kimberley Park, 91
King's Bromley, 72
King's Lynn, 82, 84: custom house, **99**, 100
Kingston, 42
Kirby, 58
Kirby Misperton, 110
Kirby Moorside, 110
Kirby Muxloe, 71
Kirby Stephen, 121
Kirkham, 110

Kirkoswald, 126
Kirkstone Pass, 122
Kirstead Old Hall, 90, Plate XVI
Kirton, 102, Plate XVIII
Knaresborough, 113, 114, **115**
Knightwick, 67
Knook, 36
Knutsford, 79
Kynance, 52

Lakes, the, 100
Lamberhurst, 6
Lancaster, 118
Land's End, 31, 50, 51
Langham, 20
Langley Castle, 127
Lanherne, 50
Lastingham, 110
Launceston, 49
Lavenham, 84, 86, 87, 88, Plate XV
Lawkland, 117
Leamington, 55
Ledbury, 57, 67
Lee, 118, and Littledale Fall, Plate XX
Leek, **79**
Leighton, 74
Leith Hill, 11, Plate IV
Lewes, **xi**, 3, 16
Leyburn, 120
Lichfield, 72
Lilleshall, 72
Lincoln, 82, 83, 84, 100, 101
Lincolnshire Wolds, map, **101**
Lindley, 115
Lingwood, 95
Liskeard, 53
Litchborough, 59
Little Brington, 59
Little Canfield, 18
Little Chishall, 26
Little Gaddesden, 26
Little Hampton, 66
Little Hautbois, 94
Little Walsingham, 91, the Green at, Plate XVI
Lizard, the, 49, 52
Llanthony Abbey, **69**
Loftus, 112

INDEX

Logan, 51
Long Marston, 66
Long Melford, 19
Long Mynd, 74, Plate XIII
Long Sutton, 99
Longridge, 118
Longstones, 31
Looe Island, 53
Louth, 82, 84
Lower Brockhampton Manor, 67
Lower Peover, 78
Lower Westwood, 39
Lowestoft, 83
Ludlow, 57, 74, **75**
Lugg, the, 67
Lyddington, 58
Lyme, 32
Lyme Bay, 31
Lymington, 38
Lytes Cary, 33

Maldon, 4, 22
Malton, 110
Malverns, the, 67
Marazion, 52
Market Bosworth, 71
Market Deeping, xvii, 98
Marlborough, xii, 33
Marlborough Down, 30
Marlowe, 3, 23
Marske, Swaledale, xxi
Marton, 78, 79
Marston, 66
Marston Moor, 113
Mathon, 67
Mawgan, 50
Meadrose, 50
Medmenham, 24
Medway, river, 2
Medway Valley, 5, 11
Melbury Hill, 37, Plate VII
Mells, 40
Melmerby, 126
Melton Mowbray, 68, 70
Mendips, the, 30, 40, 41
Mendlesham, 88, Plate XV
Meon Valley, 14
Mid England, map **70**
Middleham, 120; Castle, **121**
Middle Littleton, 66

Middleton Lodge, 116
Midhurst, 3, 4
Mildenhall, 83
Milton, ix
Minchinhampton, 63
Minehead, 42, 44
Minshull, 78
Minster Lovell, 63
Mobberley, 78
Monks Eleigh, 88
Monsal Dale, Plate XIV, 79
Monnow, river, 68
Montgomery, 75
Morecambe Bay, 107, 118
Moreton Hampstead, 46
Moreton Old Hall, **77**, 78
Morton Pinkney, 59
Morwenstow, 50
Mount Harry, **15**, 16
Mount Sorrell, 71
Mousehole, 51, 52
Much Wenlock, 74
Mullion Coves, 52
Mytton Green, **117**

Nadder Vale, 37
Nantwich, 57
Nayland, 4
Nayland, Plate V, 19
Needham Market, 88
Needwood, 55
Nether Keller, 118
Newby, 117
Newark, 56, 83
New Forest, 30, 33
New Forest, map **34**
Newby Head, 119
Newlyn, 51
Newmarket, 82, 83
Newport, Essex, 19
Newport, Shropshire, 72
Newquay, 50
New Romney, 8
Newton Flotman, 91
Newton Linford, 71
Nidd, the, 107, 113
Norfolk and the Broads, map **90**
Normanby, 104
Northampton, 59
North Barsham, 92

INDEX

Northern England, 106
Northleach, **61**, 62
North Willingham, 104
Norton St. Philip, 38, 39
Norwich, 82, 84, 85
Norwich and District, 89, 90
Norwich Way, 83
Nuneaton, 72

Oakham, 57
Occlestone Green, 78
Odiham, 4, 13
Offa's Dyke, 56, 75
Offenham, 56
Okehampton, 46
Old Moreton, 57
Ollerton, 80
Osberton, 80
Otley, 115, 116
Otterburn, 127
Ouse, the, **xx**
Overbury, 67
Owlpen, 57, 63
Oxford, 56, 60
Oxmead, 94

Painswick, 63
Pakenham, 87
Parham Old Hall, 89
Patterdale, 122
Peak, the, 55
Peak, the district, map **76**, 79
Pebworth, 66
Peddars Way, 83
Pembridge, 67
Penhurst Park, 4
Penkridge, 72
Pennines, southern, 54
Pennines, the, xvii, 106, 107, 126
Penryn, **52**
Penshurst, 5
Pentewan Valley, Plate X
Pentire Point, 50
Penzance, 51
Pershore, 57
Peterborough, 98
Petersfield, 14
Petworth, 3, 14
Pevensey, 3
Pickering, 110

Pilgrim's Way, 2, 9, 10
Pitch Hill, Plate I
Pitsford, 59
Plymouth Hoe, 32
Polperro, **52**, 53
Pontrilas, 68
Poole Harbour, 31
Pooley Bridge, 121
Poringland, 90
Port Isaac, 50
Portland Bill, 31
Portreath, 50
Portsmouth, 3
Potter Heigham Bridge, **94**
Potterne, 36
Poynings, 16
Prestbury, 78
Preston, 106
Preston Plucknett, 41
Princes Risborough, 26, Plate VI
Purbeck Island, 31, 38
Puttenham, 12
Pyecombe, 16

Quantocks, the, xiii, Plate IX, 30, map **3**
Quarry Woods, 23
Quorndon, 71

Ragdale, 57, 71
Raithby, 104
Ramsey, 97
Reading, 4
Redruth, 49
Renwick, 126
Ribchester, 118
Ribble, the, 107, 116, 117
Ribble Head, 119
Richmond Castle, 120
Ridge Way, the, 31
Ridwares, the, 72
Rievaulx, 108
Rievaulx Abbey, 112
Ripley, 113, 114
Ripon, 108, 113
Rissingtons, the, 63
Robin Hood Bay, 107, 112
Rochester, 10
Rockingham, forest of, 58, 59
Roding, Plate V

INDEX

Roding, river, 17, **18**
Roman Wall, 107, 122
Romney Marsh, 2
Rookwood Hall, 18
Rosamund's Well, 74
Rosedale, 110
Ross, 57
Rothbury, Plate XXII, 127, 128
Rother, river, 6
Rother, the, 2
Rowlands Castle, 14
Royston, 26
Rufford Abbey, 81
Rugby, 63
Rugeley, 72
Rumbles Moor, 116
Runnymede, 22
Runswick Bay, 107, **111**, 112
Rushbrooke Hall, 86
Ruston, 110
Ruthwaite, 122
Rye, 3, 6, **7**, 8
Ryecroft Gate, 79

Saffron Walden, 19
St. Agnes Beacon, 51
St. Albans, 2, 3
St. Austell, 52
St. Columb Major, 50
St. Gennys, 50
St. Ives, Cornwall, 32
St. Ives Bay, Cornwall, 51
St. Ives (Hunts), 96
St. Ives (Hunts), the Bridge, xvii
St. Michael's Mount, 51
St. Mary's, 97
Salisbury, 29, 37
Salisbury Plain, 30, **34**, map **34**
Saltash Ferry, 53
Salthouse, 93
Sandbach, 78
Sandringham, 100
Sandwich, 3, 8
Savernake, woods, 30, 33
Saxlingham, 91
Saxthorpe, 93
Scalby, 112
Scarborough, 108
Scarborough Castle, 112
Seale, 12

Sedgemoor, 32
Selbourne, 3
Selborne, **13**, 13, 14
Semley, road at, **36**
Sennen, 51
Settle, 117
Seven Wells Combe, Plate IX
Severn Valley, 54
Severn, river, 74
Shadwell Hall, 75
Shaftesbury, 37
Shaftesbury, road at Semley, **36**
Shenston, W., xiv
Shenton, 72
Sherborne, 32, 41
Shere, 12
Sherwood, 55
Shipton Hall, 74
Shoyswell, 6
Shrewsbury, xiii, 56, 72, 73, 74
Sibsey, 105
Sidford, 42
Silbury Hall, 31, 34
Silchester, 2
Simonsbath, 44
Simonside, 127, Plate XXII
Six Hills, 70
Skegness, 82
Skiddaw, 107, 122
Skipton, 117
Soar, the, 70, 71
Solway Firth, 107, 123
Somersby, 102
Somerset and Lynn Bay, map **39**
South Burlingham, 95
South Carlton, 102
Southampton, 3
Southend, 17
South Molton, 44
South Petherton, 41
South Tyne, the, 126, 127
South Wraxall, 33, 39
Spalding, 82, 84
Spalding, Holbeach Road, Plate XVII
Spilsby, 82, 105
Sparrow Pit, 79
Sparsholt, 62
Staines, 22
Staithes, 112

INDEX

Stafford, 72
Stagshaw Bank, 127
Stane Street, 3, 11
Stanton, 66, 79
Steyning, 3, 16
Stiffkey, 92
Stockton, 32
Stoke Albany, 59
Stokenchurch, 24
Stokesay, 57
Stoke-sub-Hamdon, 41
Stonehenge, 31
Stoneleigh, 65
Stoney Middleton, 80
Storrington, 16
Stour, the, 2, Plate V
Stour Valley, 19, 20, 21
Stowmarket, 87
Stratford, 57, 63
Stud Green, 78
Sturry, 8
Suckley, 67
Sudbury, 19
Suffolk towns, map **85**
Sulgrave, 59
Surrey Hills and the South Downs, **12**
Sutton Bank, 106, 113
Sutton Cheney, 72
Swaledale, 106, 120, 121
Swan Green, Plate VII

Tamar, river, 31, 53
Tame, the, 72
Tamworth, 56
Tan Hill, 106, 121
Tarporley, 78
Tattershall Castle, 84, 104
Taunton Castle, 32
Tavistock, 46
Teesdale, 126
Tees, the, 107
Teme Valley, 74
Tewkesbury, 57, 63, 66
Thames, the, 2, 22, **23**
Thanet, 2
Thaxted, 4, 19
Thetford, 82; doorway at, **86**
Thirlmere, 122
Thirlwall, 108

Thirsk, 106, 113
Thorney, 97, 98
Thornton Dale, 110
Threshfield, 117
Thurne, bridge over, 95
Thwaite, 121
Tideswell, 79
Tilbury, 17
Tilgate Forest, 16
Tillington, 67
Timbercombe, 42
Tintagel, Plate X, 32, 50
Tintern, 68
Tintern Abbey, Plate XII
Titchfield, 14
Toddington, 26
Tong, 72
Torridge, 14
Torrington, 44
Tostock, 87
Totnes, 32, 47
Tergatta, 50
Trent, the, 72
Trerule Foot, 53
Treryn, 51
Trewarmett, 50
Troutbeck, 122
Trowse Hill, 90
Truro, 52
Tunbridge Wells, 3, 6
Tutbury Castle, 72
Twycross, 72
Tyne, river, 107
Tysoe, 65

Uffington, 62
Ugley, 19
Uley Bury, 63
Ullswater, Plate II, 122
Upper Millichope, 74
Upper Slaughter, 63
Uppingham, 58
Upton Grey, 13
Ure, the, 107
Uriconium, 56, 74

Wadebridge, 50
Wadhurst, 6
Wainfleet, 82, 105
Walberswick, 95

INDEX

Wall Houses, 127
Wallsend-on-the-Tyne, 123
Walmer, Kent, 2, 3
Walton-on-Thames, 27
Wansdyke, 31, 34
Wantage, 56
Warboys, 97
Warburton, 78
Wardour, 37
Ware, 4, 27, 28
Wareham, 32, 38
Warminster, 36
Warwick, 56, 64
Warwick Bridge, 126
Warwickshire Avon to the Wye, map **64**
Washington Country, map **58**
Washington House, Little Brington, **60**
Washington, Laurence, 59, tomb, **59**
Washingtons, the, 56
Wash, the, 83, 100
Wasperton, 65
Watling Street, xii, 26, 56, 63, 72
Watlington, 4
Wattesham, 88
Weald, 1, 2
Wear Gifford, 44
Welbeck Abbey, 80
Welbourne, 100
Welford, 66
Welland River, 58, 98, 99
Wells, Norfolk, 82, 92, 100
Wells, Somerset, 32, Plate VIII, 40
Wells Stream Fen, 100
Welsh Marches, 54, 56, 75
Wendover, 26
Wenlock Edge, 54
Wensley Dale, 116
Weobley, 67
Westbury, 36
West Hoathly, 16
Weston, 116
West Stoke, 14
West Stow, 87
Weston Park, 72
Weston Patrick, 13
Westwood, 38

West Woodburn, 127
Wettenhall, 78
Weybourne, 93
Wharfe, the, xiii, 107
Wharfedale, 115
Wharfedale, Baidon Tower, Plate XX
Wharfe Valley, 106, 116
Wheathamstead, 3, 4, 27
Whernside, 119
Whitby, 112
White Horse Vale, 54, 55, 57
Whiteleaf Cross, the, 26
Whitesand Bay, 53
Whitfield, 126
Whittlesea, 97
Wickhambreaux, 8
Widemouth, 50
Widford, 3, 27
Wight, Isle of, 30
Wilderhope Manor, 74
Willersley, 68
Williton, 44
Wincanton, 29
Winchcombe, 66
Winchester, 3, 8
Windermere, 122
Windrush, the, 62, Plate XI
Windsor, 2, 22
Winsford, 44, **47**
Winterbourne Stoke, 36
Wisbech, 83
Witham, 22
Withyham, 16
Wixford, 66
Wolds, Lincs, map **101**, 102, 103, 104
Woodbridge, 89
Woodford, Cheshire, 78
Woodhouse, 71
Woodlands, Chiltern, 24
Wookey Hole, 40
Wool, 33
Wooler, 128
Woolmer, Hants, 2
Worcester, 56
Worstead, 85
Worksop, 80
Worth Forest, 16
Wragby, 104

Wreake, 70
Wrekin, the, 74
Wroxeter, 56, 74
Wroxham, 94
Wych Cross, 16
Wye, the, 55, 67, 68, 79
Wye, from the Warwickshire Avon, map **64**
Wyndcliff, 68
Wyle Cop, 73
Wylye, 36
Wymondham, 91
Wyre, 55

Yarborough Road, 102
Yarmouth, Norfolk, 83, 84
Yare, river, 91
Yeavering, 128
Yeovil, 41
York, xiii, 107, 108, 109
Yorkshire Dales and the Lakes, map **119**
Yorkshire Moors and Coast, **109**
Youlgreave, 70

Zigzags, view from, **13**

www.ingramcontent.com/pod-product-compliance
Lightning Source LLC
Chambersburg PA
CBHW050635160426
43194CB000108/1675